T0276320

# VICTORIAN
## SOUTHWEST MICHIGAN
# TRUE CRIME

# VICTORIAN
## SOUTHWEST MICHIGAN
# TRUE CRIME

*Michael Delaware*

THE
History
PRESS

Published by The History Press
Charleston, SC
www.historypress.com

Copyright © 2024 by Michael Delaware
All rights reserved

First published 2024

Manufactured in the United States

ISBN 9781467156073

Library of Congress Control Number: 2023949141

*Notice*: The information in this book is true and complete to the best of our knowledge. It is offered without guarantee on the part of the author or The History Press. The author and The History Press disclaim all liability in connection with the use of this book.

All rights reserved. No part of this book may be reproduced or transmitted in any form whatsoever without prior written permission from the publisher except in the case of brief quotations embodied in critical articles and reviews.

*This book is dedicated to the history fans who have journeyed with me into yesterday and followed my work on YouTube and my podcast* Tales of Southwest Michigan's Past.

# CONTENTS

# ACKNOWLEDGEMENTS

I would like to thank The History Press for giving me the opportunity to publish my first book in this genre. I would also like to thank all of my fans on my YouTube channel and my podcast *Tales of Southwest Michigan's Past* for their support and encouragement of my work over the years.

History Press authors Amberrose Hammond, Blaine Pardoe and Dianna Stampfler deserve a special mention for encouraging me to take the next step. They are incredible.

In the research for this project, I would be remiss if I did not mention the Willard Library in Battle Creek, its wonderful staff and historical records. I cannot thank them enough.

I also owe thanks to many people who were willing to assist me on this project. Special thanks to Carol Jones who searched museum records in Dexter, Michigan, helping me find the graves in the Butcher of Dibble Hill story.

Thank you to the Historical Society of Battle Creek for help with finding photos. Also a special thank-you to Bonnie at the Holbrook Heritage Room at the Branch County District Library for images of the Coldwater School.

Also, thanks to my friends who share my passion for local history and are my sounding board: Donna Hazel, Amy South, Al and Anne Bobrofsky, Donna Rickman, T.R. Shaw and Kurt Thornton.

Special thanks to my friend Dave Eddy for reviewing the final manuscript and offering encouragement over the years. Also to Jim Jackson who taught me valuable researching tools in genealogy.

My friend Bobbie Mathis from the Union City Society of Historic Preservation deserves a special thank-you for directing me toward the Crouch murder case and sharing her Union City research.

The Battle Creek Regional History Museum is due thanks for rekindling my passion for writing through my volunteer work with the organization. I especially want to thank Doug Sturdivant for believing in me, even when the tasks I endeavored to take on seemed impossible.

Finally, my biggest supporters have been my family. I was blessed to grow up with a father who was a storyteller and a mother who was a passionate librarian.

My brother Richard Delaware offered brilliant insight and help with editing some of the chapters herein. My sister Jeanne Matheny spent countless hours proofing every single chapter in this book, returning glowing praise after reading every story, despite the dark subject matter. Without a doubt, this book would have not been possible without her wholehearted support.

# INTRODUCTION

The Victorian era refers to the period in Western history during the reign of England's Queen Victoria from 1837 until her death in 1901. In England and America, it was a time of transition from predominantly rural agricultural economies to the height of the Industrial Revolution.

As with any time period, there are those who committed heinous crimes disturbing the tranquility of society. This is a book about true crime. All of the events described within actually happened, and the stories are told with the best efforts at historical accuracy.

In some cases, material on events was limited. Whenever possible, details were cross-referenced between newspaper accounts, biographical material, land records, birth and death records, census records, historical maps and the works of other historians from the period.

As you read through this collection of stories, it is important to note that the investigative procedures of law enforcement during the Victorian era were quite different from what we read today in novels or see on true crime shows on streaming services and television.

The usefulness of fingerprint evidence did not become known until Sir Francis Galton, an Englishman, published a scientific study on the subject in 1892. Although the police in Scotland Yard in London made use of this information following the release of the study, the method for identifying individuals was not put into broad use by law enforcement in the rest of England and America until decades later.

Queen Victoria, 1859. *By Franz Xaver Winterhalter—Royal Collection.*

In 1901, Karl Landsteiner made the discovery of the first human blood groups. Prior to that, testing for blood at crime scenes was done only to verify whether it was human or animal.

Testing of chemicals found in the stomach of a victim could be done, if labs were available, to determine whether the individual was poisoned or ingested some other lethal compound. However, knowledge of forensic medicine was limited.

Transportation in Michigan during the Victorian era was also restrictive. Travel by law enforcement to a crime scene was done by horseback, wagon, carriage or on foot.

After the 1870s, which was considered a golden age of the railroad in the Great Lakes region, law enforcement could take trains to reach locations or deliver specimens collected to laboratories at the University of Michigan in Ann Arbor if needed. Prior to that in southwest Michigan, horseback couriers, stagecoaches and carriages were used to deliver samples to the westernmost train station or, depending on the year, all the way to the lab.

The automobile would not come into broad use until the 1920s.

Communications were much slower as well. The first telegram was sent by Samuel Morse from Washington, D.C., to Baltimore, Maryland, in 1844. Although Western Union built the first transcontinental telegraph line in 1861, with over 100,000 miles of telegraph lines by 1866, even stretching across the ocean to Europe, messages required trained code users to interpret until 1914. Expansion of telegraph lines often followed the railroad, not offering access to many smaller communities in Michigan until after 1870. Getting an alert sent required someone to journey to the telegraph office and find an available operator.

Telephone exchanges did not begin to be established in communities until mid-1880, and long-distance telecommunications in Michigan did not come into broad use until the early 1890s. When someone sent for law enforcement from a rural area, this was typically done by sending a rider or a runner to notify them. Arrival time of law enforcement at a crime scene could be several hours from the time it was discovered and reported.

Compounding the problem with delays in transportation and communications was crime scene contamination. Edgar Allan Poe invented the detective story with "The Murders in the Rue Morgue" in 1841, and it was embraced by an enthusiastic readership. Inspired by Poe, Sir Arthur Conan Doyle published his Sherlock Holmes series in magazines starting in 1887, fueling a culture of amateur sleuthing during this era.

In many cases, authorities would arrive on a scene to find neighbors and journalists had already been on location for hours, gawking at the victims, trampling over footprints, collecting and disturbing evidence in an effort to find clues or "get the scoop." An extreme example can be found in the Crouch murders of 1883.

The practice of law enforcement securing crime scenes as it has evolved today, to preserve evidence, did not come into broad use until almost over a century later. DNA testing, blood splatter and body fluid analysis, hair and fiber comparison, ballistic testing, grid search patterns, chain of custody and so many other tools and methods in modern use by investigators were not even on the horizon during this time.

Detectives of this era also had limited to no use of photography until after the Civil War in 1865, when it began to become more mainstream. Although the first use of forensic photography was introduced in Belgium in 1851, the practice did not become cutting edge until the 1870s. Broad use of photography in crime scene investigation did not become common until the early 1900s.

A few of the stories within this collection were unsolved murders during their time. Perhaps if the investigators of that era had the tools of modern-day law enforcement, the cases would have been solved.

The legal process was different then as well. When it came to trials, often a lot of hearsay evidence was allowed to be admitted, which would be denied in courtrooms today. Hearsay evidence is largely inadmissible in modern judiciaries because of the inability of the other party to cross-examine the maker of the reported statement.

According to legal blogs, the history of the hearsay rule as a distinct idea began only in the 1500s in English courts and did not gain complete development and final precision until the 1700s. From the 1600s to the 1800s, the rule developed slowly, and the first rule became universally accepted in the English and American legal systems in the mid- to late 1800s.

In reviewing published testimonies of trials during this era, as in the case of the Crouch murder trial, it is clear that hearsay evidence was still permitted in the Jackson County courts in 1884. The same would hold true for many of the other trials detailed herein.

In Michigan at that time, when a man was convicted of a crime, especially first-degree murder, the punishment often included solitary confinement intermixed with hard labor. Many a convict went insane from extended isolation, aging far beyond their years when serving out their sentence.

Women, on the other hand, if convicted, were often given better treatment when incarcerated. During the Victorian era, there were two regulators of feminine behavior: society and the law. The law was written in an attempt to treat women and men equally when it came to crimes such as murder. However, the law was enforced by members of a society that did not believe men and women were alike. In many legal cases of the time, when it came to a woman on trial for murder, the jury—which was composed of men—held firm with the assumption that "female nature" did not predispose them to be capable of the temperament to commit murder. Murder was regarded as masculine behavior.

Thus, when you read the cases of Sarah Haviland and Mary Sanderson in this collection, consider their outcomes within the context of Victorian-era society. It will also shine light on why Austin Smith was charged with murder and Anna Owens was so easily exonerated.

Further, it is also important to note that during my research there were contradictory spellings of individual names between sources of written accounts. For example, one of Martin and Frances White's daughters was referred to as May in all newspaper accounts of the case. Some written by reporters who knew her, however, burial records and her headstone indicate her name was in fact Mary. The 1880 U.S. census listed her name as May, so it is likely she was called that as a nickname. Thus in writing the story, I had a difficult decision on which to use and ultimately chose the name written on her headstone.

Another example of this is in the Dall Swartz case. Most of the newspaper accounts of the time spelled his name as Del Swartz. However, a biographical account that was written by a detective who worked the case clearly spelled his name as Dall. Upon reflection, I decided to use the spelling of the firsthand account of an investigator on the case, rather than that of a newspaper reporter who may have transcribed the story from a telegraph transmission.

Also, there were some names where I decided to use the common name the person was called at the time, rather than their full given names.

Examples of this are in the Haviland Children Murders of 1865. The name of one of the sons was Ira Arthur Haviland. However, he was referred to by everyone of the time as Arthur, so that is what I used in telling the story. Additionally, I considered it might have been confusing to the reader if I referred to him as Ira, as this was also his father's name. Likewise, one of Haviland's daughters was Nancy Jane Haviland, but in all testimonies from people of the time, she was referred to simply as Jane. Thus, I chose to use what she was commonly called.

As a final note, you will find within the pages of this book that the method of murder varied from revolvers, knives, axes and razors to hammers, poison, strangulation and more. It was with no intention on my part to include such a wide methodology to murder. My research mission was to find crimes that spanned the period and the region, especially forgotten stories that received statewide and national interest in their time. It does, however, bear out as a historical truth that it is not the instrument of murder that holds any consistency, but the sinister impulse behind the criminal act wherein lies the true evil.

Michael Delaware
2023

1

# THE TRAGIC DEATH OF DORRENCE WILLIAMS (1846)

*This morning while Charles Sturgis, the sexton at Oak Hill Cemetery, assisted by Josiah M Caldwell, were removing the remains of Dorrence Williams on the cemetery lot now belonging to Daniel Clark, they made a discovery…*
—Battle Creek Daily Moon, *October 3, 1887*

Dorrence Williams came originally from Newton Township, Portage, Ohio, where he owned fifty-nine acres. He first arrived in Michigan working as a surveyor of the land surrounding the region of the Goguac prairie in 1828, long before any non-Indigenous settlers had arrived. This area of southwest Michigan would eventually be organized into Calhoun County a few years later. The community that would in time emerge first as the village of Milton, and later as Battle Creek, was still an untamed wilderness.

## SURVEYORS AND SETTLERS

The first survey conducted on the Michigan Territory of any significant import was completed in an expedition of 1814–16 by Edward Tiffin. Tiffin had been the first governor of Ohio in 1803, and in later years he was appointed as the Surveyor General of the Northwest Territory by President James Madison.

His expedition was to determine the condition of land in the vast Northwest Territory, which the U.S. government intended to give to the veterans of the War of 1812 in exchange for their service. Tiffin's report on the rest of the region, which included Indiana, Illinois and Wisconsin, was favorable. However, his report on Michigan claimed that the land was mostly swamp and unsuitable for agriculture.

The Tiffin survey deterred early eastern settlers from finding their way into Michigan, and instead they settled in other parts of the Northwest Territory. It was not until 1820 that Lewis Cass, the second governor of the then territory of Michigan, undertook a new expedition to survey the region and returned with an entirely different report based on his observations. In the wake of the Lewis Cass Expedition, the eastern and southeastern counties were organized, and Michigan began to see an influx of settlers arriving in search of new land opportunities.

Land in these new territories was offered at $1.25 an acre by the U.S. government to anyone who wished to settle there. Further, a congressional act of 1812 gave men the incentive to serve in the U.S. Army in exchange for land. Congress passed laws that established bounty land warrants to be awarded to noncommissioned officers and soldiers, or their heirs, who served in the war. Due to the Tiffin survey, initially Michigan was avoided, and settlers converged on Ohio, Indiana and Illinois and some traveled as far as Wisconsin.

It wasn't until the Erie Canal was finally completed in New York in 1825 that migration from the New England area into Michigan increased. However, within a decade of the Cass report, it was clear that an even more expansive survey was needed to organize the southwestern Michigan region into counties.

Beginning in 1828, hundreds of surveyors were contracted by the U.S. government on behalf of the Michigan Territory. They made their way into the wilderness to map the topography, trails and rivers of this region, surveying the terrain as part of this massive project to divide land into the future counties and townships of southwest Michigan. Dorrence Williams was one of the number of original surveyors, responsible for the section south of downtown Battle Creek today over to Athens.

When the survey teams had completed their work in 1830, fourteen lower counties of Michigan were organized under the direction of Governor Lewis Cass spanning from Jackson County west to Berrien County, south to the Indiana state line and as far north as Ingham and Barry Counties. Suddenly it was a more appealing route to travel from Vermont, Massachusetts and New York down the Erie Canal and across the Great Lakes to Michigan. In contrast, the land route that ran through Pennsylvania and Ohio to arrive in Indiana or Illinois, before Michigan, was arduous.

# The Goguac Prairie

If you live in the area of Goguac Lake today in Battle Creek, what was called the Goguac prairie during the time of Dorrence Williams spanned from the area of the Kellogg Airfield near Helmer Road to as far east as the Penetrator (I-194). It was a flat, grassy expanse between multiple copses of burr oak, maple and pine trees. Today, it consists of entirely residential neighborhoods.

The primary Indigenous people in this region during that time were the Potawatomi. The name Goguac may have come from a Potawatomi word *Coguagiack*, which means "waving grasses" or may describe a bowl-like depression that has water, surrounded by trees and high grasses. In either case, when Williams arrived, it was a wide, expansive and mostly unpopulated prairie. Being familiar with the region since 1828, Williams was at an advantage over other pioneer explorers who would appear in 1831. He knew where he believed the premium locations were in the area to settle and made his claim on them as soon as the land was available.

The Goguac prairie offered a fertile soil, clear of dense forest. The Native Americans burned the prairie grass seasonally to enhance the visibility of smaller game, and the rich loam was now over a foot deep across many sections of the mostly level plain. These rich conditions of the soil made it perfect for growing wheat, an early pioneer crop in this region. However, plowing through this depth of loam was not without its challenges, and many a plow blade was broken as the land was cultivated.

Despite this, the wide-open prairie was more favorable to the early pioneer than forested land that required the removal of trees, stumps and brush before one could till the soil for planting. The open prairie made it possible to sow and plant wheat, a crop that grows abundantly in most any soil, before the first winter.

Williams selected a fractional quarter of section 14, in Battle Creek Township, where he settled in the late autumn of 1831. This location is just north of Goguac Lake and today contains a commercial shopping center and residential neighborhoods. (In 1873, the land was owned by William Foster, who later sold the farm to John Stewart, who would plant the first apple orchard in the Battle Creek Township.)

Wasting no time, Williams built his log cabin on the south border of the prairie near the woods. He owned in all some four hundred acres of land, a part of it lying between the future site of the downtown village of Battle Creek and Goguac Lake.

# THE RIGHTEOUS BACHELOR

Williams had lived a determined life of a bachelor. He was described by those who knew him best as a good man. However, they also regarded him as a peculiar man. He was said to have considered himself a gentleman in the chivalrous sense of that term and held the highest opinion of his own honor. It was stated that he considered that his own word was solemn, and no man must challenge him on this. In other words, he thought himself very important, always right with his opinions, and asserted this position with others he encountered. Here we undoubtedly get a clue to the real difficulties that attended him through life.

His overpowering sense of honor, justice and right did not spare any sensible consideration for the human nature of others. His encounters with fellow pioneer citizens, along with his personal dealings with them, were described as engaging with a "pretty crooked stick at the best."

Dorrence Williams was naturally of a suspicious nature and was afraid every man he dealt with was striving to cheat him. This kept him at odds with somebody most of his lifetime. The memory of him retained by those he knew in these early pioneer settlement years was not through pleasant social encounters.

Instead, more often than not, it was an unpleasant memory of having to defend themselves in a lawsuit with Williams as plaintiff than by any other channel. As the community was established, and the courthouse built, Dorrence was a frequent and familiar face before the local courtroom judges.

The following example was described as having the distinction of never having been equaled in any courtroom.

The defendant in a lawsuit, in which Williams was the plaintiff, was testifying against him. Williams thought the man was very clearly testifying falsely.

This did not set well with Dorrence, and he rebuked the defendant loudly during the man's testimony in front of the judge with a vociferous "You lie, sir!"

On behalf of the court, the judge censured Williams, saying he would not allow such language to be used.

The indignant bachelor explained:

*Your Honor, had I said to this man*—you lie! *I ought to have been fined for contempt of court. But I said, you lie,* sir! *Which last word "sir" raised the expression from any* vulgar *meaning, and instead of slandering the man I* honored *him by its use.*

The judge, no doubt astonished at this profound distinction, after a brief pause for consideration, waived all censure. The trial then proceeded.

This was just one typical example. Williams was so often legally combative that many of his surrounding neighbors refused to have any further dealings with him. It is likely that when they saw Dorrence coming down the street, they would purposefully walk away in the other direction or cross the street to avoid an encounter.

## Encounters with Native Americans

Throughout southern Michigan and in parts of Ohio, Indiana and Wisconsin there were earthen mounds. When the settlers inquired among the Potawatomi Indians as to their origins, they did not know who made them, only that they were burial mounds from a people who lived before them in the region.

Some believe these people were distant relatives of the Sauk people, a tribe the French had encountered in 1667, which had long since been driven out of the region by the 1800s. Others claim they were an ancient Native American culture that lived originally in the Ohio valley and expanded across the Midwest region to as far north as Minnesota and as far south as Mississippi as early as 6000 BCE.

Regardless of their origins, on the four-hundred-acre farm of Dorrence Williams there existed one of these earthen mounds. The local Potawatomi had requested this mound, and others in the region, be treated with respect.

Word of this had gotten back to Williams, but he dismissed Native American concerns and once attempted to satisfy his curiosity concerning the mound on his farm by digging into it.

The Potawatomi observed him one day at work on the mound with his spade. They then threatened him to such a degree that he was afraid to remain on his land. The encounter shook him to the core, and he left Michigan and returned to Ohio in fear. He was gone almost a year before he returned. The Potawatomi were the only people who Dorrence Williams had trouble with that he did not sue.

He had returned to Battle Creek by the time the 1840 census was taken, and by then he no longer owned land in Ohio. He was recorded in the census as living with two other men but was listed as head of the household.

In 1846, at the age of thirty-nine, Dorrence Williams died at his home on the prairie. His cause of death was described as kidney difficulties. He had been struggling with an illness that lasted several days. He was found in his home nonresponsive on Sunday August 23 and was buried on August 26, 1846, at Oak Hill Cemetery.

## An Unexpected Discovery

Because the cemetery was new, just two years old at that time, Dorrence had purchased a large plot consisting of sites for several graves. Perhaps he was considering that one day he might have a large family and would need such a plot. Or perhaps it was his own sense of self-importance that drove him to do this. It is certain, however, he never expected to die so young. His death, however sad, was at the time apparently unremarkable.

Four years later, in 1850, the father of a man named Daniel Clark approached the Oak Hill Cemetery administrators in search of a large family plot in the same section as Williams's plot. As the plot was the only large one remaining in the section and no other family members of the deceased could be identified, Oak Hill Cemetery made arrangements to sell the plot to the Clarks. The purchase was made with the understanding that the remains of Dorrence Williams would be removed and interred in another smaller plot elsewhere in the cemetery.

The work to move the grave was delayed an astonishing thirty-seven years until 1887, when the sexton of Oak Hill Cemetery at the time, Charles Sturgis, assisted by Josiah M. Caldwell, finally got around to digging up the remains. What they discovered was gruesome and would be something they would remember for many years to come.

When they unearthed Williams's remains, they opened his coffin. His head, which had a remarkably thick skull, was turned to one side, in a corner of the coffin. Both hands had been brought up to the face and clenched it. The body was turned over from the way it was originally laid, and the knees were brought up under it clear to the chin. The position displayed real desperation such as a person would assume in the dread of despair, the

Dorrence Williams's headstone. *Author's collection.*

aftermath of someone who must have come to realize the true nature of his terrifying and horrendous situation.

Dorrence Williams had been buried alive! Efforts were again made to find any of his relatives, but none were found after a thorough search. Several "old residents" were asked about the bachelor, and all they would say is that they could remember there was something peculiar about his case but none could call to mind what it was.

The bones of Williams were described as being in an excellent state of preservation considering they had lain there over forty-one years.

The sexton, his assistant and all who had seen the remains were convinced that Dorrence Williams had been buried alive. The only question was whether this had been an unfortunate tragedy or a murder.

The members of the community considered it fortunate that at the time of the discovery no one of his family survived to be haunted by the terrible thoughts of his sufferings, despair and death in that cramped cell. His final hours must have been unimaginable terror.

## Secret Crime or Unfortunate Tragedy?

Were some members of the community who knew him but were less than forthcoming about Williams holding something back? Was this a mere tragedy that a man as litigious as Dorrence Williams within this small community, who seemed to make more enemies than friends in life, came to experience such a terrible end? Or was there something more to the story that will remain a mystery lost in time? Was there some hidden plot to get back at Williams for all of his unceasing lawsuits? Did he push someone too far with his litigations?

There are more unanswered questions regarding his death than anyone will ever find answers for.

In the 1800s, medicine was not as advanced as it is today. Seriously ill people slipping into a coma could have easily been taken for being dead. It is quite possible this was the sad fate of Dorrence Williams.

Today, if you are curious, you can find Dorrence Williams's gravestone close to the fence on the north side of Oak Hill Cemetery, about two hundred feet from the corner of the east fence. It stands a lonely vigil over his second and final resting place.

# 2

# THE CAPTAIN AND THE AXE MURDERER (1848)

*That he [James] who has thus acted, is more than ever entitled to our esteem and confidence, and that he who has the moral firmness to withstand the promptings of the natural ties of brotherhood...*
—*the citizens of Marshall, 1848*

James Winters was born in Chenango, New York, in 1805. Growing up, he learned the trade of a cooper, a maker of wooden barrels. He moved to Marengo Township, just outside of the village of Marshall, Michigan, in 1836, with his wife, Theodosia, seeking better opportunities in the new territory, like so many early pioneers.

He settled nicely into the growing village and, from 1839 to 1842, managed his own small farm. In addition to these labors, he worked as the foreman of a large cooper shop in Marshall. During his time there, he became involved in the community, even serving a one-year term as the coroner in 1841. This was during a time in history when a medical degree was not required for the position, but a knowledge of carpentry often proved to be useful.

## A RESPECTED CITIZEN

James later moved to the Athens, Michigan area, settling in the adjacent Leroy Township with his family and acquiring a ten-acre farm. He also continued his work as a cooper there.

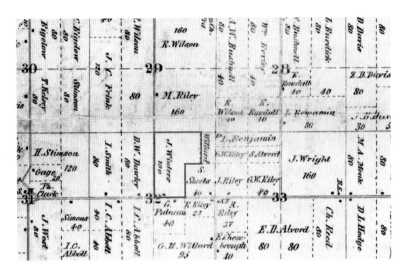

James Winters's farm in 1858. *U.S. National Archives.*

In 1844, he was elected as the township supervisor, a position he would serve in for several years. His election was driven by a spirited and rising Whig Party in the area. During this time, the two political parties in the United States were the Whigs and the Democrats. The Whigs favored an economic program known as the American System, which called for federal subsidies for the construction of infrastructure, protective tariffs, congressional regulation on the expansion of slavery and the support for a national bank, all issues that were largely opposed by the Democrats. However, the principal differences were that the Whigs believed that the legislature should have the most power in government, whereas the Democrats supported a strong executive branch.

In his position as supervisor, James also became the acting justice of the peace. In addition, he held other township offices over the years, including postmaster of the Pine Creek Post Office in 1851, a locale that was a small collection of homes not far from his farm. Additionally, he was among the group of pioneer founders of the Baptist Church in Athens, where he served faithfully as a trustee.

James earned some notoriety within the community by being the first to own a threshing machine, which he purchased in 1840 and brought with him to Athens from Marshall. It was an open cylinder machine and required quite a bit of labor to work with. Many during his time considered it disagreeable and even dangerous to work around. However, James was the sort of individual who was always willing to try something new and embrace a difficult task in hopes of future benefit. It was this tenacious characteristic that gained him admiration and respect from members of the community.

## John Winters

James had a brother named John Winters, who also migrated from New York and settled in the community of East Leroy near Athens. He had established a small farm not far from James's house, separated by a small forest of burr oak trees and scrub pines.

Older than James by a few years, John was a man of seemingly opposite character to his brother. Where James was openly interested in working with members of the community, John was more guarded, fostering suspicions of others. Despite this, James and John were fairly close as brothers, both having taken the journey to Michigan from their home state of New York around the same time in 1836.

In November 1846, at the age of forty, John married Linancy Ludden, who was thirty-eight years old. She was born in Athens, had grown up there and was very outgoing and social with members of the community. For the first year of their marriage, all seemed to be in harmony with the newlyweds.

However, in the spring of 1848, John began mentioning to friends within his sphere, in confidence, that he suspected his wife of unfaithfulness. Witnesses would later testify that they considered his claim against her groundless and dismissed it whenever he would mention it. Nonetheless, John let these suspicions simmer in his soul.

My mid-April, the flames of jealousy had begun to occupy his thoughts continually. Convinced of his wife's treachery, his internal torment caused more ebb than flow in civility toward her. Bitterness entwined with loathing and boiled into barely restrained rage.

## Betrayal

On April 25, 1848, he told Linancy that they should walk over to his brother's house and visit with James and Theodosia, then stay the night. Before leaving for their walk, John picked up his axe. He told her that he needed to bring it along so that he could sharpen the blade using the stone at his brother's house.

Their path took them along a trail through the woods of about a mile or more, between the two homesteads. They started walking at around three o'clock in the afternoon. The skies were clear, although there was still a late spring chill in the air. Early leaves on the trees were emerging with their familiar green and gold.

When they reached the halfway point between their two houses, on the most secluded portion of the trail in the woods, John discreetly drifted back behind his wife and let her take the lead. Letting loose his pent-up rage, he then swung the axe at the back of Linancy's skull. The blade struck her with such force that her head cleaved open like a gourd with that single brutal stroke.

Linancy tumbled headlong to the ground. Whether she cried out in pain is not known. Walking up to where she had collapsed just off the trail, John struck another blow to the side of her head with the flat side of the axe.

His wife lay unmoving with her skull fractured severely, brain matter exposed and protruding through the massive rupture. Her limp figure lay among the bushes and vines on the forest floor. He made no effort to bury or conceal her body. He simply walked back the way they had come, axe in hand, abandoning her to scavengers and decay.

## DISCOVERY

She was discovered at six o'clock later that same day by a young boy named Putnam who'd been out wandering in the woods. To his astonishment, this mutilated woman was still alive and even moaning when he found her. With haste, he ran home for help. She would at length be moved by neighbors to a doctor's house nearby.

To make her as comfortable as possible, Linancy was laid in a bed. She would remain in a state that was described as "insensible," drifting in and out of consciousness the rest of the night. Still breathing, but unable to communicate, she writhed the remainder of the evening. Linancy Winters ultimately passed away at around one o'clock the next morning.

When Linancy was discovered, township authorities were notified and a constable called to investigate. James Winters was still the township supervisor when this incident happened, and as mentioned earlier, he served as justice of the peace. He could have used his authority to dismiss any investigation or charges against his brother but instead he stood by his own moral character and did not interfere as they traced the blood trail that dripped from the axe back to John.

Perhaps he suspected the temperament of his brother, or maybe it was the shock of seeing firsthand the mutilated body of his sister-in-law. Whichever it was, he cast aside any personal bond he may have had with his brother and, sustaining the integrity of the law and his authority, remanded the investigation to the county.

John Winters was found to be in possession of the axe used in the crime and was apprehended. He was taken to Marshall to be held in the county jail awaiting an inquiry and ultimately a trial.

# THE TRIAL

The case of the *People vs. John Winters* took place in May 1848. Many witnesses for the defense testified on John's behalf as to his character. Most were relatives, along with a few other citizens who knew him from the Athens community. James's reputation had, in many respects, been extended to John over the years. The defense attorney, a Mr. Gordon, attempted to use this testimony in hopes of John receiving a lesser charge of manslaughter.

However, James refused to support his brother in his defense. He had been, like so many other members of the community, shocked and appalled at his brother's alleged actions. He was not willing to deny his own morality to ease any punishment that might be forthcoming toward John, should he be pronounced guilty. He stood firm on his abstention from participation in the trial.

The prosecutor, Mr. Pratt, despite the defense's best efforts, offered an irrefutable case. He presented the axe, the testimony of the physician who examined the victim and that of the boy who found her, as well as of the others who carried and attended her in her final hours.

The prosecution also presented witnesses who testified to John's statements concerning his suspicions of Linancy's infidelity in the weeks prior to the incident. Tales of his orations about his building jealousy in the month preceding the murder would unravel any hope for leniency.

After only a very short deliberation, the jury returned with the verdict of guilty of murder in the first degree.

Judge Miles, after expressing a few feeling and impressive remarks, sentenced John to solitary confinement along with hard labor at the Michigan State Prison for life. John Winters was taken by coach to Jackson the following morning.

The citizens at the trial, most of whom were acquaintances of James from his time living in Marshall, observed the proceedings as they unfolded. Disturbed as they were at the brutality of the crime, they uniformly respected James Winters for standing by his own moral integrity and not supporting his brother's defense team.

In fact, from the time his brother was arrested, James made no attempt to interfere with the legal process. He ignored pleas and promptings from his brother to use his position within the community to help him avoid prosecution and having to face justice.

After the conviction, witnesses to the trial presented a card to James Winters, signed by many prominent members of the community expressing sympathy toward him for the distressing circumstances of his brother having committed such a crime. Among the many names who signed were Isaac Crary, Charles Gorham, Oliver C. Comstock, Samuel Hall and Reverend John D. Pierce, all leaders, professionals and successful businessmen in Marshall.

The card's inscription read:

*Whereas, the recent trial and conviction of John Winters, has necessarily brought deep mortification upon the family and friends of the prisoner, we the undersigned friends and acquaintances of Mr. James Winters, our respected fellow citizen, cannot in justice refrain from expressing this publicly, our deepest and heartfelt sympathy with him at this distressing event, and take this occasion to acknowledge what the public universally concede; the high minded and honorable course pursued by him, to vindicate and sustain the character of the laws in affording every faculty in his power to the public authorities to bring to justice and punishment, the guilty offender, and that we view it as no ordinary mark of a high minded, pure and virtuous man, and that such conduct confirms our opinion, that he who has thus acted, is more than ever entitled to our esteem and confidence, and that he who has the moral firmness to withstand the promptings of the natural ties of brotherhood, dear as they are engrafted in the human heart, to perform his duty to God and his fellow man, is indeed an upright citizen, and that such acts should receive as they deserve the approving voice of the community.*

# The Captain

James Winters would go on to serve as a representative of Athens in the Michigan state legislature from 1853 to 1854. In the 1860 census, he listed his trade as a shoemaker, an indication that he moved away from farming and expanded his business interests even further.

In 1861, he raised a company of one hundred men and became captain of Company E, Sixth Michigan Infantry, at the start of the Civil War. He resigned, however, soon after organizing the company due to ill health. Despite this setback, he would carry the title of Captain Winters the rest of his days.

His Sixth Michigan Infantry unit served victoriously at Baton Rouge and later at Port Hudson. A few years later, he drilled officers of the Thirteenth Michigan regiment, preparing them also for war.

James would continue his trade as a cooper and shoemaker, as well as a farmer, for many years in Athens. In 1862, his daughter Rosalba was born, and she would grow up in the Athens community.

In 1869, James contributed the chapter "A History of Athens," published in the Calhoun County Business Directory for 1869–70, under the byline of Capt. Jas Winters. This article detailed much of what is known today about the early founders of the village.

James remained a respected and honorable citizen in the Athens community, and the incident with his brother faded from memory. He again served as justice of the peace in 1879. He passed away in January 1882.

# The Axe Murderer

John Winters, on the other hand, began his incarceration at the Jackson Penitentiary. He was reported to have attempted escape during his stay there; however, he was not successful. He remained in solitary confinement, only taken out for hard labor, which was in accordance with his sentence.

On November 23, 1859, the officers of the prison solicited Governor Moses Wisner on his behalf, to obtain his release, and he was eventually granted a pardon. At that point, he was described as an old man who had been confined to his cell for over ten years. He never returned to Athens, nor did he ever reunite with his brother.

# 3

# THE MURDER OF JOHN WILEY (1855)

*The house of R.W. Pendleton, in this village, was the scene of an affray on
Tuesday evening last.*
—Democratic Expounder, *November 15, 1855*

In Marshall, Michigan, on November 13, 1855, shots rang out at the
home of Reuben Welton Pendleton while he was away on business in
Chicago. The events of that evening would leave one man dead and
another man sentenced to life in prison.

To the residents of the city at this time, the tragedy that night was
shocking and initially somewhat of a mystery. The trial that unfolded in
the coming months would add clarity to all that led up to the incident—a
story that Reuben Pendleton would have preferred to have been kept in
confidence. It was a tragedy brought about by infidelity and driven by the
tempest of jealousy.

## OLD JOUR

Reuben Pendleton was a cabinetmaker who owned a brick house in Marshall,
which was described as a handsome property. He was originally from
Connecticut and was known as "Old Jour" Pendleton among his friends, a
nickname from his early days as a journeyman in his craft. His first wife was
Sarah Ann Darling, who died in April 1848 at the age of thirty-one, leaving

him with two children. He married again that same year to twenty-year-old Caroline Pringle. Reuben was thirty-six, and together they had a son.

Reuben occasionally took on boarders, renting out rooms for extra money. One boarder who took up residence was John Wiley, a somewhat wild and frolicking engineer, who worked for the Michigan Central Railroad. He arrived in Marshall in August 1855.

## THE CHARMING ENGINEER

John was apparently quite the charmer. Instead of just renting the room and going about his business, he took an interest in Caroline Pendleton, whom he began addressing as "Kate." The two began to engage in "unlawful intimacy," as extramarital lovers' trysts were described in the mid-1800s. It wasn't long before Reuben discovered their secret.

Reuben ordered John to leave the house and forbid him from returning. John responded by saying, "I will visit Kate, whenever I take a notion, and the devil can't stop me." This insolent response only further infuriated Reuben.

John Wiley did leave the house and went to stay with a friend from the railroad by the name of William Plummer on September 4, 1855. He returned with Plummer to pick up his trunk, guns and other personal effects the following day. Plummer said that he remained living with him and on occasion would sleep in the train cars, which was part of their job.

Mrs. Pendleton did not want anything to do with Reuben's decrees concerning John Wiley. Whenever Reuben left town, John Wiley would stop by to visit, often at her invitation. Reuben suspected this was happening, and in November 1855, when he had to go to Chicago on business, he gave his brother Increase Pendleton and a friend, Dewitt Horton, a key to his house. He instructed them to keep an eye out for Wiley. He urged them if they found Wiley inside the home to alert the county prosecuting attorney, John Van Armen, with whom he would leave instructions.

## THE TRIO ON WATCH

They watched the house for several nights, recruiting another man named J.K. Byers to help them. On a Tuesday night, November 13, three days after Reuben had left town, they detected that Wiley was indeed inside the home with Mrs. Pendleton.

Wiley wandered over, not telling his friend William Plummer where he was going. Mrs. Pendleton invited him in when he stopped by for a visit.

The three men approached the house with the intention of entering and arresting John Wiley. Horton was armed with a Colt revolver pistol. He had been advised by Reuben not to go to the house unarmed, as Wiley was known to carry a double-barrel shotgun and a pistol.

They placed the key in the door, only to discover the keyhole had been filled with lead. They therefore broke the door down and entered. There was a loud crashing noise when they did this, on top of shouting out Wiley's name. As soon as they entered, the candle lights in the foyer were suddenly extinguished.

## Melee in the Foyer

DeWitt Horton, the first inside, was immediately knocked down by someone unknown in the darkness. A melee broke out in the dark foyer, and someone struck Horton in the eye with a chair. Wiley had extinguished the lights in the foyer when he heard them coming in, retreating upstairs. He threw down a chair, which struck the first man inside.

Horton had charged in with tremendous force and was several feet into the foyer when he was hit. He retreated eight or ten feet backward, drawing his pistol. Wiley was holding a light in one hand, waiving a chair leg in the other, at the top of the landing, and charged down the stairs. Horton fired several shots at Wiley, with one bullet striking him in the stomach. Wiley, when he made it down the stairs, struck Horton with the chair leg. Byers interceded and delivered some blows to Wiley.

By then, the shot that struck Wiley in the abdomen was taking effect. He doubled over. Sheriff Harvey Dixon was called and arrived at the scene. He described the foyer as being scattered with fragments of chair all over the place. Horton had cuts on his face, and one eye was swollen.

Dixon went over to Wiley and asked him if he had been shot. He replied, "Yes, in the bowels. I have been given a death blow."

Wiley told him what had happened. He said that Horton had rushed in and began ascending the stairs, and he had asked him what he was coming up for. Horton had replied, "By God, I'll let you know!"

He claimed that was when he threw the chair that broke across Horton's face. Then he charged back downstairs, and Horton shot him.

# Investigation and Trial

Different witnesses testified to various accounts of the events that evening. Some claimed the crash of the chair came at the same time as the gunshots. Others claimed the crash came first, then the gunfire.

Initially, Dixon arrested DeWitt Horton, J.K. Byers and Increase Pendleton and took them to jail. J.K. also showed signs of having been in the fight. Increase, it was confirmed, did not enter the home and had remained outside. He was initially charged as an accessory but later released before the inquiry hearing.

John Wiley saw a doctor, and the bullet was removed. However, his intestines had been pierced, and medicine during this time was not so advanced. He died a short time later, likely from internal bleeding or infection. His body was returned to his family in Richland County, Ohio, and buried in Mansfield Cemetery.

The inquiry that followed aired out the affair that John Wiley had with Mrs. Pendleton, Reuben Pendleton's conflict with his wife and instructions to his brother and DeWitt Horton. During the hearing, Mrs. Pendleton was put on the stand, but she refused to answer questions. She was sent to jail for several days with the charge of contempt of court. As a result of this hearing, Byers was released and Horton was charged with murder.

The trial was held in December 1855, with John Van Arman representing the defense of DeWitt Horton. The trial lasted several weeks, and the jury was sent out for deliberation on December 25, Christmas Day. They remained in their room for only about an hour and returned with a verdict of murder in the first degree. Van

John Wiley's headstone. *Krista Cameron, Find a Grave.*

Arman immediately filed an appeal, but the Michigan Supreme Court ruled against his client.

In January 1856, Dewitt Horton was sentenced to state prison for life. He served only three years in prison, receiving a pardon by Michigan governor Moses Wisner in 1859.

# 4

# MURDER ON THE PLANK ROAD (1855)

*He said that as they drove on, she would say every time the wagon jolted "Oh, Tim, don't kill me."*
—Marshall Statesman, *May 7, 1856*

The early roads in the pioneer era of southwest Michigan from 1829 to 1845 were known as the Territorial Roads or Pioneer Trails, which stretched east as far as Ypsilanti and to the west arriving in St. Joseph. These were often narrow roads filled with wagon ruts, carved out through the many years following the original footpaths made through the wilderness by the Native Americans. Traveling on these roads was often tedious and slow, obstructed by rocks, fallen trees, marshes and mud.

Early solutions were to build corduroy roads, consisting of logs laid side by side across marshy areas, secured with crossbeams. These worked fairly well, when most of the travel on these roads was primarily wagons pulled by sure-footed oxen. However, as travel by horse became more common, corduroy roads proved to be hazardous to the equine traveler. Corduroy roads could shift or separate, resulting in hooves falling between circular logs and horses receiving injuries.

# PLANK ROADS

The next-best solution the early pioneers could come up with was a wooden highway made of logs hewn into planks. Timber was in abundance and considered valueless, so it was an easy resource for building roads.

In 1848, forty-six plank road companies were chartered in Michigan. In 1849, thirty-nine companies were chartered; then in 1850, sixty more plank road companies were chartered. One could easily refer to the period from 1845 to 1855 as the plank road era in the state of Michigan, as there were well over one hundred companies organized to build these types of roads.

In 1849, the legislature incorporated the Battle Creek & Hastings Plank Road Company with the authorized capital of $40,000 to build a plank road from Battle Creek to Hastings. The road was constructed. For many years, it was the main toll road between the two cities, primarily traveled by horseback, wagon, carriage and stagecoach. Tolls were set up at various intervals along the road, and the revenue generated was returned to the stockholders of the plank road companies, when privately funded, or to the municipality.

This plank road was the main route through Bedford, Michigan, from Battle Creek, as one traveled to Hastings. It is also the setting for a tragic murder that happened in 1855.

A plank road in the late 1800s. *U.S. National Archives.*

# A Long Day

On December 5, John Burns was walking on the plank road on his way to Battle Creek from Bedford Township. This route follows along what is today Michigan Avenue. It was ten o'clock in the morning, and he was four or five miles from Battle Creek.

Heading in the same direction, coming from behind, was a wagon filled with a load of wheat. Driving the team of horses was a woman, Bridget Dunn. Walking alongside the wagon was her husband, Timothy Dunn. As they passed Barney's Tavern, a stagecoach stop in Bedford, about a half hour later, they said hello to the tavernkeeper's son Oliver Barney. All were in good spirits on this cold December morning as the wagon caught up to Burns on the road.

Timothy Dunn walked alongside Burns, engaging in social banter all the way to the toll booth just outside of Battle Creek. They stayed at the booth for about fifteen minutes, paying their tolls and talking with the toll keeper, William Sudbury. Here Burns observed Mr. and Mrs. Dunn having a drink of liquor, he from a flask and she from a glass provided by Sudbury. When they departed, Timothy Dunn climbed aboard the wagon and invited John to ride along the rest of the journey, which he did.

They parted ways when arriving in the city and agreed to meet up in the evening and ride back together. The Dunns then continued onto the granary and sold their wheat. While in town, they visited several stores, making purchases.

They also met with two men, John Lowry and George Grossback, to settle some business. Timothy Dunn owed Lowry one hundred dollars, and he paid him. Their meeting location was a saloon called the Hole in the Wall. Both would later recall that both Timothy and Bridget Dunn had some drinks during their meeting between four and five o'clock.

An hour or so later, Lowry ran into the Dunns again while passing a boardinghouse owned by the Devault family. He witnessed them later having drinks with the patrons. He remembered they both seemed in good spirits.

John Burns encountered Bridget in the late afternoon with some parcels in her apron, with Timothy following behind carrying a bag of nails.

When Burns met them later for their return trip to Bedford, the wagon was loaded with bags of goods, including flour and three or four bushels of lime. A hay knife lay beside the bags, along with some other crockery supplies. In the 1850s, a hay knife was an elongated straight or slightly curved blade, similar to a handheld sickle, often with one or two ninety-degree-angled

Examples of different types of hay knives. *Author's collection.*

handles. It was used for cutting wheat and hay. The edge of the blade in such an instrument was quite sharp, and the width was usually about three inches.

There were two boys in the front of the wagon this time driving the team homeward, and Mr. and Mrs. Dunn climbed into the back with Burns. When Timothy Dunn got into the wagon, he pulled out a flask of whiskey and handed it to Burns, who took an obliging drink and handed it back. On the return journey in the wagon, he did not see Bridget drink, but he recalled Timothy was drinking considerably. He described them both as being very pleasant and good-natured.

When the wagon reached the toll station, Timothy went inside the house to pay. There he met with William Sudbury, the toll keeper, and asked him for some whiskey, drinking this time from an offered glass. While he was waiting outside, Burns took the hay knife out of the back of the wagon, concerned that someone might cut themselves in the darkness when climbing back in, and placed it on the front board of the wagon, laying the blade flat.

Mary Sudbury, the toll keeper's wife, had invited Bridget inside when they arrived, offering her some tea. She observed that Bridget appeared somewhat tipsy and tired. She offered the Dunns their guest bedroom to stay overnight. However, they declined the invitation and resumed their journey home to Bedford. Mary would later recall that they both seemed to be about to tip over, as they walked unsteadily back to the wagon.

John Burns parted ways with the Dunns when the wagon came in proximity of his home shortly after passing Barney's Tavern. The two boys who were driving the wagon also ventured off to their respective homes. The Dunns continued on toward Bedford on the plank road alone, and Timothy took over driving the wagon with Bridget sitting beside him.

# FALLEN WOMAN

About a mile west of Barney's Tavern, after Burns had left their company, John Hawes, traveling on foot on an intersecting road, encountered the wagon between eight and nine o'clock in the evening. It passed in front of him on the plank road ahead. He hastened to reach the intersection, hoping to catch a ride.

He heard groans from a person and dogs barking from a nearby farm when they went past. At first, he could not see whether it was a wagon or a carriage. When he reached the wooden road, he heard a loud sharp sound like a stone being thrown against the box of a wagon, heavy and hard. It was dark, and the sound came from the direction the vehicle had gone. When he emerged onto the plank road, the moon was now shining bright from behind the trees. He saw it was a wagon that had stopped a little farther down.

He walked straight toward it.

When he drew closer, he saw a woman lying on the tracks of the road, behind the wagon. The woman lay partially on her side, with her head pointed toward the back corner of the wagon.

A man stood over her, next to the wheel of the wagon. The man, seeing Hawes approach, said to him, clearly drunk: "Here is a woman who fell out of the wagon."

Hawes responded: "Get her into your wagon and take her home."

The man replied: "No! I'll be damned if I do! Damn her, I dunno her, I dunno her!"

Then he leaned over the woman and said in a drunken stupor: "Old woman, where you going? Where you come from? Where you going?"

Hawes, now recognizing the couple in the moonlight, looked at Timothy Dunn and said, "It is your wife."

Dunn responded, "I'll be damned if it be her! I'll leave her for some farmhouse," implying he would just leave her for a local farmer to find.

Hawes replied, "You cannot leave her here."

Dunn said, "I cannot get her into the wagon."

Hawes told him, "I will help you then," and with this, he took hold of the woman's arms. Dunn grabbed her feet, and together they lifted her into the wagon. Hawes noted that the woman made no sound and said nothing to him, even though he was close to her face in the darkness when he lifted her.

However, Hawes did not consider the idea that she might be dead. Being familiar with the couple, he assumed they were both drunk and she had just fallen out of the wagon.

Before Dunn drove off, Hawes told him to cover up Bridget so that she would not catch cold. Dunn responded gruffly: "No! Damn her, she won't take any harm."

Hawes saw that the woman's knees were exposed to the cold, so he reached over and covered them up with a horse cloth that was in the back of the wagon as best he could. Hawes would later relay the experience to another neighbor on his way home that night, William Edget. He explained how Dunn tried to tell him he had just come across an old woman, who was really his wife, on the road and wanted to leave her for a nearby farmhouse and head on his way.

Dunn did not offer Hawes a ride but just got in the wagon and drove the horses with a good stroke, riding off into the night.

# Lost After Dark

He first arrived at the home of a neighbor, Elisha Carpenter, when his horses turned into her yard. Elisha came outside when she heard someone talking very loudly.

As soon as Dunn saw her, he yelled out, "Where am I?"

Elisha replied, "You are in my yard."

She then offered to go inside and come back out with a lantern to show him the way home. Dunn stood outside by the horse until she did this. He had driven into her yard, which was about a mile before his own house after the plank road had turned north. Elisha Carpenter owned almost two hundred acres bisected by the road, now known as Collier Avenue.

Returning with the lantern, she directed him where he needed to go. When he turned the wagon around, Elisha observed Mrs. Dunn lying in the back, and alongside her lay the hay knife. Assuming Bridget was asleep, she said to Mr. Dunn, "I will remove this and place it in the front, so she does not get cut."

Timothy Dunn stopped her, retorting, "Damn her! Let her get cut!"

Elisha then stepped away and walked to the head of the horses to point them in the right direction. She told Mr. Dunn the horses would be able to find their way home. He came over to her and reached up grabbing the harnesses, asking her if the harnesses were all right.

When he did this, she saw that his hand was dripping with blood, as if it had been dipped into a bucket. In the light from the lantern, she also saw there was blood on the hay knife.

Dunn climbed onto the wagon and looked at her, saying, "I have seen more trouble tonight than I have seen before in five years! I am a poor damn drunken Irishman! My mother never brought me up to do what I have done!"

With a snap of the leather, he directed his team across a little hollow, where Elisha had pointed, saying "Hallo" to her as he drove off.

Elisha, in shock at what she had seen, gave no reply. When she turned to go back inside her home, echoing in the night, she also heard William say loudly to his wife: "Are you dead? Are you dead?" as his angry voice faded away in the dark.

# The Irishman's Bad Business

When Timothy Dunn arrived at home, their twenty-one-year-old daughter, Mary, greeted him outside along with her nineteen-year-old brother, Barney. She observed her mother was in the back of the wagon, lying straight, with her face up. She did not know what she was lying on in the dark. She thought perhaps it was her shawl. There were bags of lime at her feet that had been loaded in the wagon, along with a sack of flour, and crockery supplies they had purchased in town.

Mr. Murphy, a neighbor, and John Dunn, her uncle, and his wife, along with her brother, Barney, carried Mrs. Dunn into the home. They placed her beside the fire, leaning her up against a chair. She did not move after being brought inside the house. Barney would maintain that she was alive when she was carried inside, as he had heard her moan.

Timothy tried to get Bridget to drink some tea, but she was not responding and the liquid just ran down her lips and face. Barney became visibly upset seeing his unresponsive mother and began pacing around the room crying.

Everyone in the house at this point assumed there had been some kind of accident, where Bridget, while intoxicated, had fallen out of the wagon. This was how Timothy had presented it when he arrived.

Barney was sent by Timothy to summon a local nurse, Mary Hamilton. When she arrived, she saw Bridget was not moving and assumed she was dead. Her face had been washed by Timothy Dunn by the time Mary Hamilton had arrived. The nurse observed a noticeable cut on the other woman's forehead over one eye, below a sizable bruise on her head. She also found there was a cut on her forearm between three and four inches long.

Mary Hamilton had Timothy assist her in carrying Bridget to another side of the house, and they lay her down on a board. She did not notice any blood where Bridget had been lying but noticed the blood drizzling along behind them as they carried her. She also saw blood under her dress, around her hips. She erroneously concluded it was menstrual blood, as it looked lighter in color, so she made no further examination.

Mr. Fuller, another neighbor who came by, would later relay that Timothy Dunn said to him while Mary Hamilton was examining his wife: "Mr. Fuller, this is bad business. Had I known this would have happened, I would not have gone to Battle Creek. I am the rascal, and I ought to be shot."

# INVESTIGATION

After a time when it was determined that Bridget was dead, the coroner was notified, and an official inquest was organized. An inquest during this era consisted of men appointed by the coroner to investigate the events leading up to a person's death. It included medical doctors and also members of the community if no constable was available. As part of this investigation, a preliminary medical examination of Bridget Dunn was completed that evening.

The doctor discovered the laceration and bruising above her eye; the cut was one and a half inches deep. There was also a contusion next to her nose and bruising on her neck and right collarbone and under her right breast. As mentioned before, there was a laceration on her arm. There were also bruises on the back of her right hand and on her right hip, along with more bruises on her thighs.

The bleeding from under her skirt was caused by a three-inch-deep incision on the inside of her right thigh just above the knee, about four inches long.

Dr. Simeon French. *Historical Society of Battle Creek.*

The doctor determined the cut had been made with an elongated cutting instrument, consistent with a hay knife.

He also concluded that a blow with such force against the head, and other areas, might be enough to knock a person into insensibility, producing a state of bewilderment, with the possibility of causing them to lose balance and fall. He concluded that some of the injuries were caused by the knife, a blow to the head and also the fall from the wagon.

Further examinations by two medical doctors, Dr. Simeon French and Dr. Edward Cox, discovered a much deeper and severe wound in the area of her vagina, also consistent with being stabbed with the same elongated instrument.

The justice of the peace, G.W. McAllister, recounted later his interview on the night of December 5 with Timothy Dunn. Dunn related how he and his wife traveled to Battle Creek that morning at ten o'clock, and while in town he had purchased a hay knife, a bottle of whiskey, crockery and other supplies. When he went to the grocery, he drank some alcohol and later had some brandy at another location, plus two to three drinks at the saloon.

He said that Bridget had drinks as well but claimed she was sober when they left Battle Creek. He could not recall whether he had some more alcohol at the gatehouse when he paid his toll, but William Sudbury claimed he had. He said that his wife fell out of the wagon somewhere between the gatehouse and Barney's Tavern on their return trip.

He had not stopped immediately to pick her up because he was "vexed" with her. She had been complaining the entire journey when he was driving every time he hit a bump and the wagon jolted. She would exclaim, "Oh Tim, don't kill me," when hitting some of the bigger ones.

This made him angry, and he wished to punish her. When McAllister pressed Dunn on when Bridget had been making these statements, he claimed it was after they had parted company with the other passengers.

The examining medical doctors, French and Cox, would testify at trial that the cold weather would have slowed the bleeding and swelling but maintained the internal injuries to Bridget would have been fatal.

Another physician, Dr. Nicholas Maniates from Marshall, Michigan, was also brought in to testify at the trial. He confirmed the wound to her vagina would have been a more vascular injury and likely caused internal bleeding. He said the ragged laceration indicated it was done by the push of a long end of a sharp instrument, consistent with the end of the hay knife found in the wagon.

The prosecution also brought four other physicians—Dr. Henry Joy, Dr. John Howard Montgomery, Dr. Paul Church and Dr. Joseph Sibley—from Marshall to testify in their professional opinions; all four confirmed they believed the wounds were made from the hay knife.

Although his defense brought testimony from neighbors who had seen Timothy Dunn later that evening and claimed he was not intoxicated, the evidence of the injuries to Bridget could not be disproven. Timothy had been the only person in the wagon with her when she was injured, and his own statements to witnesses that evening clearly relayed he had been angry with her.

Whether driven by an alcoholic fury or not, he had struck Bridget with the hay knife and stabbed her at least twice. The cut on her arm was likely a defensive wound, in an effort to stop the assault. She had clearly tumbled out of the wagon onto the hard wooden plank road, most likely before she was stabbed.

As they were both riding in the front of the wagon when they left the toll station, it is likely that Timothy became angry with her when she complained of the jolting bumps on the road. The hay knife was lying in the front at his feet, and he picked it up and swung it at her, knocking her off the wagon, causing the cut and bruises on her face. He then pulled to a stop in front of her and got out. In his rage, with the hay knife in his hand, he wanted to inflict personal harm to her. He stabbed her in her groin area, at least twice, while shouting at her. He then threw the hay knife in anger into the back of the wagon, which caused the loud stone sound against the box of the wagon John Hawes heard when he was approaching.

Bridget's injuries to her head were likely caused by the first blow. The bruising on her body resulted from the fall off the wagon. The cut on her arm was most likely from trying to defend herself from the second blow of the hay knife when he stabbed her under her dress in the groin. It was a purposeful and vengeful personal attack to degrade her, and the outcome was fatal.

## Convicted

The jury deliberated for three and a half hours on Friday May 2, 1856, returning with a verdict of murder in the second degree. The presiding judge, Pratt, sentenced Timothy Dunn to hard labor at the state prison for twenty-five years, and Dunn was conveyed to Jackson, Michigan, the following Monday.

He was pardoned by Governor John Bagley in 1875 on account of ill health after spending almost twenty years in solitary confinement.

# 5

# THE RISE AND FALL OF OLD STARK (1857)

*He had threatened to kill her and smash her head many times. Sometimes he had good streaks. She treated him well. She called him names sometimes. She called him the Devil.*
*—Eliza Laughead,* Marshall Statesman, *March 10, 1858*

Among the many iconic buildings from Battle Creek's storied past, the first hotel has quite a history. It was known far and wide in its time as the Battle Creek House. Many a traveler on the territorial roads found lodging within, as it was close to the halfway point between Detroit and Chicago. For decades, it was the primary stagecoach stop in the area for any westward journey.

## The Center of Social Life

The hotel was built in 1838 by Leonard Starkweather Sr. on a lot he had purchased from Sands McCamly on March 7, 1837. It was located on the central intersection in the old downtown, where Capital Avenue and Michigan Avenue cross today. Back then, Michigan Avenue was known as Main Street, and Capital was known as Jefferson Avenue.

Verandas ran around the entire building on the first and second floors facing each street. On the corner of Main Street was the office, and also on the Main Street side was the sitting room. On the Jefferson Street side was the dining room, and on the second floor above was the dance hall. The rest of the building was dedicated to rooms to rent for the wary traveler.

A 1907 article in the *Battle Creek Moon* reflected on the old Battle Creek House: "One feature of the old hotel that during its time will never be forgotten by many of the 'old boys,' and that was the bar. They smile knowingly now when they speak of it, and say that in those days whisky was only three cents a glass, and it was the 'real thing.'"

Leonard Starkweather made his way to Michigan along with so many former soldiers and sailors who now converged on the region filing claims for land, as detailed in chapter 1.

He arrived in Battle Creek in 1835 with his wife, Esther Brewster; his son; and three daughters. He purchased 250 acres of farm land just north of Goguac Lake in Sections 14 and 15. Esther passed away in September 1838 shortly after he had built the hotel in downtown.

In 1839, Leonard Sr. married again to Sally Toland, the thirty-eight-year-old daughter of Canadian Isaac Toland, who had built one of the first cabins in the area, which served as a tavern, in 1831. Sally and Leonard Sr. had twin sons: John died at birth and James followed at two years old.

They had another son, Henry Clay, who drowned in June 1850 in the Battle Creek River at age five. Every year on the anniversary of his son's death, Leonard would venture over to the bridge where the boy had been found after being in the water six hours. He would look out at the river and

Battle Creek House rendering, 1857. *Willard Library Archives.*

speak with his son until the grief overtook him, and then he would return home by way of the tavern.

Tragedy would continue for Leonard, as two of his daughters from his first marriage with Esther also died from illness: Hannah at age twenty-two in 1844, and Lucia at age thirty-five in 1853. His son Leonard Jr. moved to Iowa and established his own farm, and his other daughter Lucinda married and moved away to Galesburg, Michigan. Wanting to raise their own child together, Leonard and Sally adopted a two-year-old orphan named John in 1851.

Over the decades, the Battle Creek House was a prominent fixture as the center of social activities in the community. After the election of 1850, a bonfire was held in the crossroads outside in the intersection, and the balcony was used to deliver speeches, while people gathered in the street.

In 1854, Horace Greeley—one year after the Michigan Anti-Slavery Society was formed—lectured in Battle Creek at the Methodist church. He stayed at the Battle Creek House, and his room was thronged with visitors from the local citizenry anxious to pay their respects to the man whose principles they favored. Over the years, there were many landlords, but Starkweather remained the property owner.

The hotel owner became known among the townsfolk as "Old Stark" and also "Uncle Stark." He was described as an excitable man who often spoke with a lot of hand gestures when he was trying to illustrate a point. He was known to be passionate about only a few subjects, mainly those surrounding religion and politics. Otherwise, he was regarded fondly as an amiable citizen.

The Battle Creek House was the primary location where the townsmen congregated to talk about the weather, the crops and, in later years, the progress of the Civil War. The young men gathered on the front veranda in armchairs on summer evenings to gossip. In the winter evenings, they hosted dances, oyster suppers, magic lantern shows and other entertainments. All shows were followed by a dance.

Many a pioneer could recall boys rounding up the hotel bus, which was a large stagecoach wagon, and riding around town to pick up all the girls to bring them back to the Battle Creek House for an impromptu dance in the dance hall on summer evenings.

The Battle Creek House was the main stop for the stagecoach in town, where both teamster and traveler resorted. It was nearly midway between Detroit and Chicago, on the old territorial road, and from it, the line of stagecoaches went north to Grand Rapids, west to Kalamazoo or south to Coldwater.

Historian A.D.P. Van Buren described the Battle Creek House as a place where many political meetings were held and where many battles between Democrats and Whigs were decided. He described the dances held there: "The Battle Creek House afforded an opportunity to read the character and spirit of the people during the early days. The pioneer townsmen were wont to meet in its hall and 'trip the light fantastic toe.'"

On Sunday evening, June 6, 1861, the hotel was badly damaged by fire. A valiant effort by a group of young firemen volunteers was credited with saving it. Many of this group would a short time later go off to serve in the Civil War. The hotel was repaired, having suffered only minimal damage as a result of their efforts.

While Starkweather remained the owner of the building for most of the years of its existence, there were several landlords who managed day-to-day operations. The earliest was John Henry, followed by John Wolfe and then another man named Vanderburg and several others.

The only known tragedy that ever happened at the hotel was when "Boge" Pew, the son of landlord Reuben Pew, died by suicide after shooting himself in the head behind the hotel one evening.

In 1865, following the surrender of General Lee at Appomattox, two rebel soldiers, Elihu Warner and Lucius Sweet, were made to swear allegiance and kiss the American flag on the Battle Creek House balcony. By 1865, however, the building had begun showing its age and was a stark contrast to other brick buildings in the town.

For its thirty years of existence, the Battle Creek House was the center of social activity in the community. It held its place of prominence from the early days of the village to the end of the Civil War. After 1850, Leonard Starkweather ceased being involved with the day-to-day operations of the hotel, leaving it to the landlords. Instead, he ran a small boardinghouse with his wife elsewhere in town.

On Friday, December 11, 1857, the respectable and nostalgic reputation of Old Stark came to an end within the community. On that winter evening, the tempest caged within him that heretofore had seldom emerged erupted into an unbridled rage. This was the night he brutally murdered his wife.

# Murder

A shadow fell on the Battle Creek House, even though the crime occurred elsewhere in town, as it was owned by the man who committed this heinous

Lydia Street in the city of Battle Creek, 1858. *U.S. National Archives.*

crime. The outrage of the crime shocked the community, as everyone knew Old Stark and his wife Sally.

Leonard and Sally Starkweather had a quarrelsome relationship. The incident took place in their home, which served also as a boardinghouse, on the corner of South Division and Lydia Streets. Today, Lydia Street no longer exists, having been absorbed during the construction of I-194, colloquially known as the Penetrator.

In 1857, Leonard and Sally lived with their adopted son, John, who was now eight years old. Sally also had a daughter who was now twenty-five, Eliza, from a previous marriage. She had been about eight years old when her mother married Leonard. Eliza herself had married when she was seventeen, to William Laughead, who died four years into their marriage. She had been living on her own the past three years.

The Starkweathers had three rooms rented out to boarders, a much-smaller scale than the expansive Battle Creek House in downtown.

Eliza Laughead had been at the Starkweather residence that day. She had known Leonard Starkweather for twenty years since her mother had married him. Eliza had rented a small room in the back of their home for three years and would visit with her mother, Leonard and her stepbrother John daily. She had recently moved out, but often took tea in the afternoon with Sally. She had been there for just that at five o'clock in the evening that December day and had stayed for supper.

Sally complained to Eliza of not feeling well but did not send for a physician. She did her own work at their home tending to guests, and prior to this day, in general, had always been known to be in good health.

After tea, around six o' clock, Eliza went across the street to visit another woman, Harriet Snow. When she left, Leonard Starkweather was at home, sitting alone in a chair by himself in the living room, idle and brooding.

Eliza was still at Mrs. Snow's shortly before nine o'clock in the evening, when she was called home by a young lady who said she heard some noises at her mother's house. She went directly over and walked through the front door. The little boy, John, was sitting at the dining room table, and she saw Mr. Starkweather coming out of her mother's bedroom.

Through the doorway behind him, she could see her mother lying on the floor with blood on her face, flickering in the candlelight from two candles on a table in the room.

She immediately fled, running back outside, yelling, "Murder!"

After she successfully alerted the immediate neighbors, she collected herself. She turned and went back inside to better assess the condition of her mother. Entering the bedroom, she observed that her mother was lying on the floor with her feet under the stove. Initially, she did not see the club, which was later found to be lying on the floor a few feet away. Her attention was exclusively on her mother. The club, in later reports, was also described as a baseball bat.

While standing over her mother, from behind her, Mr. Starkweather said to her: "Eliza, I have killed your mother."

This was a phrase that Leonard would repeat over and over again that evening.

Saying nothing in reply, Eliza left the house again, and went across the street to Mrs. Snow's. She sent word to the village to get the constable and this time returned with Mr. Snow to avoid being alone in the house with Leonard. She met him at the gate this time, outside the home, and he spoke again, imploring her, "I'm afraid, I have killed your mother."

Eliza again ignored Leonard and went back inside. This time she found John standing over her mother, whom she discovered to still be alive. She said, "Mother, can't you speak to me?" as blood covered her nose and face. For a moment, Sally raised herself on her elbow and then fell back down. She would pass away twenty minutes later from the trauma of her injuries.

It was then that Eliza first observed the club. John, who was standing nearby, picked it up and showed it to her. He told her it was what his father had used to kill his mother. He had witnessed the entire assault. There was blood on the club and all about her head and shoulders. There was also an empty basin now beside Sally and water all over the floor. John, in an effort to wake his mother, had filled a basin in the kitchen and poured it out on her.

Meanwhile, Mr. Starkweather had gone into another room and changed his clothes. It would be revealed at trial that Leonard and Sally, although living in the same house, had been living apart in separate rooms for the past year, as their marriage had deteriorated.

John had stayed in the same room as Sally, which was next to the kitchen, sleeping on a smaller bed that was shoved underneath hers when not in use during the daytime.

It was John who had discovered the wood that would become the club, along with another boy when they were out exploring in the nearby forest. They intended to carve it into a baseball bat, as it was naturally straight and almost exactly the right length. John struggled with getting the bark off the wood to carve it and had given it to his father, who offered to help him peel it off at the local cooper shop. He had lost track of it around the house in the past month as a young boy's forgotten project.

Since their marriage, Leonard had been known to make threats to Sally, even threatening to kill her, but according to the neighbors who knew them, he had never physically harmed her.

Eliza, however, knew of many instances from her childhood where he had done just that. One time, just a year after they were married, when Eliza was a little girl, he had kicked Sally down a hallway following an argument. In the prior weeks, Sally had shown bruises around her neck to Eliza, telling her that Leonard had choked her. Leonard was nearby and heard her relay this account to Eliza and never denied it.

Eliza also reported that her mother called Leonard names and sometimes referred to him as the devil in his presence. During the Victorian era, this type of insult was regarded as severe, especially among devoutly religious people. Leonard had always maintained outwardly to others a persona of being very pious. The two were often arguing, engaging in name-calling and lobbing insults at each other.

The man serving as constable during this time was Ogden Green, who was also the sexton at Oak Hill Cemetery. When Green arrived at the Starkweather house that evening, Leonard told him what he had done. He told Green that he thought his wife had a knife, which was why he had struck her. No knife was found on or near Sally, but one was lying on the kitchen counter.

Constable Green interviewed John, who had been present during the assault. He also spoke with neighbors and friends who had known the Starkweathers to get the details of the turbulent relationship.

# The Trial

Following the investigation, Leonard Starkweather was arrested and charged with murder. The trial held a few months later was one filled with controversy, holding a great deal of conflicting testimony. Some blamed Starkweather and others Sally for the incident, as strange as that may be to contemplate.

In an effort to offer impartiality at trial, jurors were selected from other parts of the county to hear the case. Four men from Albion, four from Sheridan Township, three from Eckford and one from Marengo Township formed the twelve-man jury.

The Starkweather trial began in March 1858 in Marshall, Michigan. The proceedings lasted two weeks.

John, who was now nine years old, had witnessed the attack that December night. He described at the trial that on the Friday night of the assault, he had eaten supper with Mr. and Mrs. Starkweather and Eliza. After eating, he had gotten his books and had a study lesson at the table in the dining room. Eliza left for Mrs. Snow's house, and his father, Leonard Starkweather, left the house shortly after.

Later in the evening, after nine o'clock, Leonard returned. John was now in his smaller bed in their room next to the kitchen, and Sally Starkweather was in there as well. Leonard walked in and took off his coat, vest and pants, stripping down to his undergarments, and then lay down on Sally's bed. She picked up his clothes and threw them out into the hall, telling him to get out.

Leonard got up and opened a broom closet, reached in and grabbed the handle of a club that was in there. He pulled it out and struck Sally, who screamed aloud when he did so. He then threw the club on the floor. John screamed too. Leonard then picked up the club again and struck Sally four more times. Two of the blows hit her in the face, one breaking her nose, and the others were to her body.

John climbed out of his bed and crawled out of the room on his hands and knees. There was candlelight in the kitchen when his mother was beaten, and John could see all of it. After the second assault, Leonard dropped the club again.

John seized a bucket of water and a bowl from the sink and poured water on Sally. Leonard told him to grab the camphor oil, which was a bottled oil often used to reduce swelling. After John returned with the oil, Leonard shouted at him to run for the doctor.

John recounted that Leonard was saying "Sally, dear, do get up," over and over again. Mrs. Starkweather was now lying between the stove and the wall. John ran to the home of Dr. Simeon French in the village to notify him he was needed. He returned just before Eliza did. John described how Eliza had gotten Sally to rise up on her elbows before she lay back down again for the last time.

The prosecution presented through testimony of witnesses that Leonard had attempted to beat Sally nine years earlier while living at her brother's house using a similar club-like instrument. He also had a history of drinking and choking her.

Dr. French testified to the injuries found on the body of Sally Starkweather, which included fragments of wood imbedded in the open wounds on her face. These indicated the force in which the blows had been delivered.

John Van Arman, a well-known attorney from Marshall, assisted by Leonidas Dibble, served as defense counsel for Leonard Starkweather in his trial. They depicted Sally Starkweather as being the aggressor, arguing a case for manslaughter, rather than first-degree murder. In the 1850s, being found guilty of first-degree murder usually came with a life sentence, whereas a conviction of manslaughter was typically less than eight years based on the law written in 1846.

The defense also brought forward witnesses who testified to seeing Mrs. Starkweather using that same club on her husband about a month earlier when she had discovered he had left the back door open. The two were reported to be almost equal in size and physical strength and frequently quarreled.

Dibble and Van Arman argued that the deed was done in a fit of insanity, driven by delirium tremens from Starkweather's addiction to alcohol. Leonard maintained a detached indifference throughout the trial, at times not betraying the least emotion, apparently unconcerned about the events unfolding before him. At the trial, Starkweather claimed he had drunk liquor three times that day and blamed his rage on the alcohol and the abuse from his wife.

Eventually, he also presented a great display of grief on the stand during his testimony, saying that he loved his wife. This was used by the defense team to persuade the jury to sympathize with him and thus lessen the charge to manslaughter.

The courthouse in Marshall was crowded every day during the trial, as Leonard Starkweather had been a longtime resident of Battle Creek and the county, and the case was considered a very important one by the press.

In the end, the jury deliberated for seven hours and returned with a conviction of manslaughter. He was sent to the Michigan State Prison and released after serving eight years.

Headstone of Leonard Starkweather. *Author's collection.*

Leonard Starkweather never returned to Battle Creek. Instead, he relocated to the home of his son in Monroe, Jasper County, Iowa, following his incarceration. He died at the age of eighty-three in February 1866. His body was returned to Battle Creek for burial at Oak Hill Cemetery. Today he rests between his first wife, Esther, and his second wife, Sally, whom he murdered.

# The Tinderbox

After Leonard Starkweather went to prison, the Battle Creek House was bought in foreclosure by William Brooks, a former mayor and merchant in town. In later years, he sold it to other investors, each taking less and less care of the building.

The old hostelry had well served its purpose, being the headquarters of all the stagecoaches leaving the city for Hastings, Grand Rapids, Kalamazoo and Coldwater. It entertained quite royally weary travelers of those days.

Finally, after the village had grown and become a city, it appeared more and more dilapidated in contrast and was not in keeping with other business structures being erected. A relic of pioneer glory days gone by, the old hotel was regarded as a blight on the downtown district.

The hotel was vacated by the last landlord, William Page, after Old Stark's death in 1866. The people in town so rejoiced on that night that several hundred invaded the old tavern and held a jubilee, marching about the rooms, hopping on the bar tops and romping around the dance hall. They were singing, blowing horns and dancing in celebration, so general was the feeling against the old structure as an eye-sore to the city.

Three months later, the Battle Creek House was totally destroyed by a fire on a Saturday night, May 5. In those days, the volunteer fire department consisted of the steamer, Union No. 1, and Tempest hand engine No. 2, each with a hose cart. There were no horses to pull the steamer. Instead, it was hauled by men with drag ropes. People standing by generally were so glad to see the old building burn that no attempt was made to save it.

The firemen working that evening were doing so only for the protection of the surrounding property. Despite their best efforts, the fire spread to other buildings before it was contained. William Green's meat market adjoined the hostelry and was destroyed along with a shoe store and another grocery store along Jefferson Avenue. However, Theodore Wakelee's dry goods store on the opposite side of the meat market was saved.

The burning hotel and the other buildings made a fire that lit up the entire heavens and was seen for miles around Battle Creek. Many farmers hitched up their horses and came into town to watch the spectacle. During the blaze, several young men who had become intoxicated attempted to cut the hose of Engine No. 1 company. A bloody fight followed in which Ed Vandemark, the foreman of the volunteer firefighters, finally used a spanner hose on the group, which effectively cleaned out the whole crowd.

In the aftermath of the blaze, some implied it might have been a merciful arsonist who set the building on fire, as many merchants long wanted to see it torn down. It was said that some person, who will never be known, died with the secret in his breast, having set fire to the old building. It being constructed of wood, it ignited like a tinderbox.

Before the smoke had cleared the air on that spring evening in 1866, the incendiary fire was forgotten. Like Old Stark, the Battle Creek House had drifted into memory, and the city moved on.

# 6

# THE HAVILAND CHILDREN MURDERS (1865)

*Why do those in trust, or those that we have in trust over murderers,*
*seem to pity a mother, who for the sake of a man's advice*
*would murder those three innocent little ones?*
—*anonymous letter to the editor,* Saline Observer, *June 15, 1895*

This story begins in Ypsilanti, Michigan, when a nineteen-year-old Sarah Rathburn married thirty-one-year-old Ira Haviland, a farmer, on July 5, 1846. The ceremony was conducted by a neighboring farmer, Prince Bennett, who served as the local justice of the peace. They resided in Augusta Township in Washtenaw County, just south of Ypsilanti, living the life and hardships of early pioneers on a forty-acre farm.

Their first child, Charles, was born in 1849. He died one year later. They would go on to have four more children, William in 1850, Jane in 1852, Phebe in 1854 and Arthur in 1858. Ira passed away after twelve years of marriage, when Sarah was still pregnant with Arthur. Ira was forty-three years old, and the cause of his death, although lost to history, may be something to reflect on when examining the events that followed.

Sarah Haviland was now a widow, alone with four children. She was described as a woman of average height, rather slightly built with jet-black hair and blue eyes and a broad, high, well-developed forehead, along with a mouth and chin indicative of firmness. Her countenance carried traces of a discernible high and fiery temper, while her manner was quick,

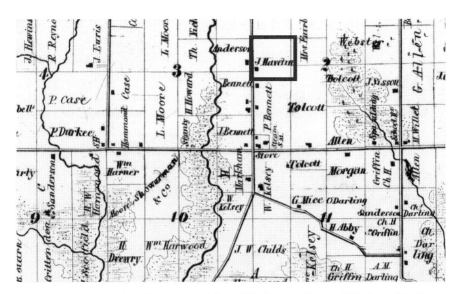

Ira Haviland Farm depicted in the 1856 Atlas of Washtenaw County. *U.S. National Archives.*

observing and intelligent. She was characterized by those who knew her as being a determined individual once she set her mind to something.

Sarah would rebound from the loss of her husband in a mere three months' time and marry again, this time to an Irish immigrant farmer named John Leonard in 1859. He would take over operation of the farm Ira had established, although perhaps not with the same vim as his predecessor. Together they had two more children, John H. Leonard Jr. in 1859 and Mary Elizabeth "Libbie" Leonard in 1861.

They lived in a Quaker community, and Sarah became involved with a Spiritualist group in Ypsilanti. She attended frequent meetings and was emerging in her role as a medium. Her involvement with the Spiritualists, however, was not agreeable to her new husband.

John was a drinker and not a very hardworking farmer according to letters from neighbors that were published in later years. Their three years of marriage were not blissful, and neighbors claimed that she would often conveniently call on their homes at mealtimes and convince the unexpecting host to prepare her children food. In the spring of 1865, Sarah left with the children in the middle of the night.

She found refuge in the use of a house owned by a man named William Phillips in Ypsilanti. Continuing with her exploration into Spiritualism, she hosted meetings at home and invited a woman named Jenny Forsyth to move in with her and the children. Difficulty then arose with Phillips, not because of the added occupant to the home, but because Forsyth was a known prostitute. He arrived to speak with Sarah about the matter, only to witness Forsyth bidding goodbye to a male customer. After being confronted by Phillips, Sarah moved out the next day.

While still in Washtenaw County, Sarah consulted lawyers and filed for a divorce. She had initially been promised by her lawyers that she would gain some property when the divorce was settled, and could sell the land and have money. With this hope in mind, she made her way west, settling in Battle Creek.

She would later claim she selected Battle Creek because of the educational programs in the community. She had hopes of obtaining the benefits of lyceum for her children. "Lyceum" refers to a hall of public lectures, an educational movement during the late Victorian era and post–Civil War period. There was also a growing Spiritualist movement in the city, with a large Quaker population.

Ultimately, she did succeed with her divorce but gained no property or money when all legal matters were resolved. John acquired the farm. After her divorce, Sarah returned to using the name Haviland. She settled in a rooming house in Battle Creek with her six children, and the stress of economics would soon require her to make other plans.

## Spiritualism in Battle Creek

Spiritualism in the United States began in 1848 in Hydesville, New York, when two young sisters, Catherine "Kate" and Margaretta "Maggie" Fox, inadvertently turned harmless pranks played on their Methodist mother into a national movement.

Kate was eleven and Maggie fourteen when they started with tying an apple to a string and letting it bump on the floor at night, making strange noises every time it rebounded. Their mother did not understand the source of the noise, never believing her young daughters would play such a prank.

They later evolved their invisible noisemaker into a story of being the spirit of a dead peddler who had died in the house. They devised a clever way to "speak" to this spirit, through rapping noises when sitting around a table. This further convinced their mother and neighbors that someone had died in the house.

Their mother, disturbed by this, sent Kate to live with their sister Leah, who became convinced of their authenticity. Maggie was sent to the home

MISS MARGARETTA FOX.     MISS CATHARINE FOX.     Mᴿˢ FISH.

The Fox sisters (*left to right*) Maggie, Kate and Leah. *By N. Currier (Firm)—Library of Congress*.

of their brother David. Leah had Kate demonstrate her skills to a Quaker couple named Amy and Isaac Post, who were longtime friends of the Fox family. They became convinced that the phenomena were genuine as well.

Word began to spread that the girls were mediums, and several public séances were held in 1849 that made them famous.

Spiritualism took on a life of its own, driven by the Quakers—the radicals of their time, pressing political issues such as abolition, temperance and equal rights for women into the mainstream. The public séances expanded to New York in 1850, attracting notable people such as James Fenimore Cooper, Horace Greeley, Sojourner Truth, William Cullen Bryant, George Bancroft and William Lloyd Garrison, among others.

As the Fox sisters' events became larger spectacles, sometimes hosting gatherings for hundreds of people, Spiritualism began to rapidly spread to other parts of the country.

This fever inspired a Quaker couple, Reynolds and Dorcas Cornell, who had purchased property on the Bedford plains west of Battle Creek, to embrace the movement. Their oldest son, Hiram Cornell, who attended Olivet College, also became inspired.

Hiram returned home from college in 1850, advancing the idea of establishing a Spiritualist school on his father's property, the Bedford Harmonial Seminary. It also became known as the Bedford Harmonial Institute. The seminary building and a large dormitory were erected. The students who would later attend referred to the dormitory as the Band Box due to it being a big three-story square wooden building. The Cornells later platted a village, using a land surveyor, christening it Harmonia.

Battle Creek, having a large congregation of Quakers during this time, saw many followers become Spiritualists. Séances were held for years at the institute. Although Harmonia never really grew to a large size in population, many students attended the institute.

Spiritualism saw a sharp rise in popularity during the American Civil War. This was attributed to two major factors, the first being the loss of so many men in the conflict, and the parents, wives and children who remained behind not always learning their fate. The second factor was advancements in photography, bringing graphic photos of fields of dead soldiers and the harsh conditions of the wounded.

Spiritualism promoted the ability to speak with the dead. A country grieving and reeling from loss yearned for what this new movement offered.

Spiritualism, however, had its critics. One of the most vocal was the magician Houdini, who denounced all of it as parlor tricks meant to deceive people.

It was during this rising wave of popularity in 1865 that Sarah Haviland arrived in Battle Creek, continuing her involvement with Spiritualism.

# Dr. Baker

Dr. Daniel J. Baker was a local leader in the Spiritualist movement in Battle Creek. He was described as being a tall, slim man of about forty-two years of age, with black hair and quite heavy black whiskers, small eyes dark blue in color, with a light complexion.

As it would bear out later, Dr. Baker was not a physician. He used the title in his practice of Spiritualism, traveling between Harmonia and Battle Creek. Most of the people he saw were involved in the movement. He was said to never have dispensed medicine but occasionally offered liquid remedies of his own creation.

Shortly after Sarah's arrival in Battle Creek in the early summer of 1865, she arranged for her oldest son, William, then fifteen years old, to stay with family in New York. He lived in Battle Creek for only a few days before moving out of state.

Sarah moved into a house owned by the Packer family behind Upton's Grocery in downtown with the rest of the children. The arrangements were confining. She made a new acquaintance, Lizzie Merritt, who would later live with her to share costs and help her with the children.

It was not long after Sarah's arrival in Battle Creek that she met Dr. Baker, who made an impression on her. She began to actively attend meetings, séances that they referred to as "circles." Her association with him soon grew into something more than mere friendship. He eventually offered financial support, and she accepted.

# The Shanty

In November, she moved again, this time to a house that was described as a low shanty one story high just south of a carriage shop. It was located near the railroad tracks, off South Jefferson Street (present-day Capital Avenue across from the Full Blast water park).

The shanty was boarded inside and out, no lathing or plastering, and had large cracks in the walls. There were two rooms, one larger than the other. There was one bed in the large room and a lounge in the other with some beds on the floor. There was no door on the large bedroom, just partitions between the bed and the ones on the floor.

Sarah shared the large room with her four younger children, Lizzie Merritt and another woman, Hattie Hannis, who lodged there only part of the week. Her oldest daughter, Jane, thirteen years old, was allowed to live on her own in a hotel in Battle Creek, near the depot. She was considered old enough to support herself with domestic work, a common practice in this period. Jane made frequent visits to the shanty.

When in Battle Creek, Dr. Baker would stay at the house and sleep on the lounge. He did the laundry for everyone in the house, sometimes the largest part of the work. He would also go into town and buy breakfast, lunch and supper for everyone there and later do the dishes.

Sarah performed any other housework needed, along with sweeping the floors. The relationship between her and Dr. Baker, although unusual for the time, never seemed to raise the suspicions of those around them.

They held Spiritualist gatherings in the shanty. These sessions included Sarah, Dr. Baker, Lizzie Merritt, Hattie Hannis and a few other followers who stopped by from the neighborhood. It was during these circles that Sarah began to take on a more central role as a medium. She would portend to be in a trance, speak to the dead and deliver spiritual messages to the living. The children were sequestered in another room, instructed to remain quiet.

Sarah later revealed that she wanted to marry Dr. Baker. When she proposed the idea to him, he was agreeable but presented to her the only bar to her achieving that goal: her three younger children. The oldest remaining with her at this point was Phebe, who in Dr. Baker's view was a good child. The other three, however, Arthur, John and Libbie, were trouble. He referred to them as "dark spirits."

Arthur, John and Libbie were rambunctious children. They constantly played loudly in and around the shanty. This annoyed Dr. Baker. Thus Baker made it clear, regarding marriage, he did not want them around. As their relationship grew, Sarah and Dr. Baker formulated plans to travel and proselytize Spiritualism around the country. They wanted to take with them Phebe and offer the same to Jane, who was becoming independent. They planned to travel the country to become national leaders in Spiritualism.

But what to do about the other three children?

# The Sinister Plan

In early August 1865, they appeared to have created their sinister plan while Sarah was still living at the Packer house: murder the children through poisoning. They would use their influence in the circles to convince all who attended that the children were "called to the spirit world," and then bury the bodies and leave town.

In August, while still in the Packer house, the three youngest children were reported to all have become sick for three days at a time. They were again unwell in September for longer periods of time, even up to moving into the shanty in November. The children complained of stomach pains and seemingly recovered.

Sarah purchased sulphur, cream of tartar and arsenic and mixed the three into a bowl with some molasses. She began administering this to the children in short doses starting in August, continuing through November, allowing them to recover for a time.

In October, Dr. Baker had a conversation with a fellow Spiritualist, Mary McAllister, saying that he had information from the spirit world that the children were going to be sick and pass away before cold weather came. He alluded especially to the three youngest children. He would later mention this same revelation to others who lived in Harmonia.

Mary had another conversation with him a few weeks later. He mentioned to her that he and Sarah were going to travel. When she inquired about what would be done about the children, he replied, "They would be taken care of one way or the other."

Mary also stated that while visiting the family at the Packer house, Sarah also offered her the same revelation of the children dying before cold weather came, adding that a spirit named "Big Indian" had told her so when in a circle under his influence. Mary recalled Dr. Baker had later told her, "You can't fool this old Indian much," and laughed when he said it.

Mary McAllister also claimed to witness Dr. Baker being abusive to the children, telling them to leave the table at mealtime, saying they were "making pigs of themselves," and hearing him once say he "would take their hides off." Other witnesses made similar allegations of Baker alluding to the children being a financial burden that would soon end.

On Monday morning, December 11, 1865, at the shanty, Sarah gave Arthur, John and Libbie each a spoonful of this mixture with arsenic before sending them outside to play. They were outside only ten minutes before they returned, complaining of stomachaches. Libbie vomited, and Lizzie held her head to comfort her, but nothing else was done for them. Dr. Baker had left earlier, heading to Harmonia for the day.

Lizzie Merritt later testified that the children, although sick, were not complaining of any pain but were constantly thirsty. She observed that night that Sarah was taking care of the children by covering them up and giving them medicine and food. Lizzie did not know what the medicine was, but she saw Sarah mixing it up.

Hattie Hannis described the mixture as being yellow and thick as molasses. When she questioned Sarah on this, she said it was for the scrofula, a form of tuberculosis.

Had Hattie consulted a medical doctor in town, she would have learned that scrofula symptoms typically involved an inflammation of the lymph nodes, not a stomach ailment.

Sarah gave the children another dose of "medicine" late in the afternoon, and they said they did not like to take it. Sarah made no answer but was stern. They reluctantly took the doses. They drank water and sat down on the lounge. Soon they began to vomit again. That evening, the children continued to complain of stomach pains. Their nausea continued, vomiting again and again.

On Tuesday morning, Lizzie asked Sarah what she was giving the children while administering a spoonful each. Sarah told her it was sulphur to "cleanse the system." Lizzie did not hear her refer to what ailed the children other than they were "much diseased."

Dr. Baker had again left for the evening. Upon his return, he consulted with Sarah about the children but said nothing more.

On Wednesday morning, Lizzie got up and observed the three children lying on the floor in front of the stove. Dr. Baker was outdoors getting some wood. The children continued to vomit most of the day. She mentioned that Dr. Baker at one point gave them some water out of a cup but never witnessed him give them any of the medicine. Sarah continued to administer the "medicine" herself throughout the day.

Hattie Hannis remembered how Sarah paced most of the day around the home with her head down, not saying much of anything.

That evening, there was a Spiritualist circle in the home. The children lay in the next room. Dr. Baker, Sarah Haviland, Hattie Hannis, Lizzie Merritt, Mary McAllister and a Frederick Windgate, from the local community, were the participants that evening.

Windgate looked in on the children when he arrived. Two were lying on the lounge; another was resting on a trunk. He witnessed the two boys vomiting a yellow liquid and inquired whether Sarah had taken them to see a doctor. Sarah said she always doctored her children herself, that they had been much sicker in the past and gotten well.

During the circle, Sarah portended to be in a trance, channeling the spirit of "Big Indian." She then proclaimed, "I know papooses sick, and they are going to the big bunk."

The word *bunk*, of course, meant they would die.

She made violent gestures, speaking in the voice of the spirit, while covering her eyes with her hands. She began dancing. She jumped up and down violently, settling down only after she claimed the spirit left her.

After briefly sitting, she claimed to be under the influence of another spirit, this time her dead brother, who repeated the warnings about the children dying. The other attendees were disturbed by this, believing in Sarah as a medium. No one dared question her on these revelations.

Their session that evening lasted only about three-quarters of an hour, much shorter than the usual three to four hours. As if by an uncanny timing, during their circle meeting when Sarah revealed the revelations of "Big Indian," one of the children vomited loudly.

After the circle concluded, Windgate, concerned, urged Sarah again to seek a physician for the children before he left. The rest of the members of that meeting remained in the house that night.

On Thursday, William, returning on a train from New York, arrived for a visit. Jane also came by, remaining in the shanty all day tending to her ill siblings. By this time, the three children were all sick in bed.

## The Crime Exposed

Lizzie stated that Dr. Baker went into town and had breakfast, returning two hours later. He then departed for Harmonia. At about six o'clock that evening, Libbie died. The Spiritualists used the phrase *passed away*, as it meant to them that someone had gone off to a continued existence in the "spirit world."

That evening, Sarah was up most of the night, Lizzie as well. Lizzie tended the fires, offering to help stay up with the two boys. Sarah insisted she go to bed. Frequently through the night, Lizzie woke up to see Sarah giving a teacup of medicine to the boys. Once, Arthur cried out for water.

On Friday, Sarah was the first one up and around the shanty. Lizzie did not recall anyone else around that day other than Jane, herself and Sarah. The two boys vomited that morning. Johnny passed away at around ten o'clock. Arthur passed away some twelve hours later that evening. Lizzie was present when he died, as were William and Phebe. They had all lain down to rest and were roused by Arthur crying out for his mother. Arthur saw his mother in tears and told her not to cry. She moved next to him, sitting there until he passed away.

The three children were then dressed in their best clothes and laid on a sheet in the smaller room, near the stove. Dr. Baker began digging a hole outside the shanty.

Earlier in the week, Lizzie had asked Dr. Baker, "If the children should die, what shall we do with them?"

He replied, "For my part, I don't know. There are boards and nails left from the shanty, if she chooses, she can take those and make boxes. Bury them in the lot."

Following this, Sarah was said to have chimed in: "If the children all die, I would not call on the county to help if they were all buried in a dry goods box."

Lizzie would later recount that the conversation had struck her as odd, and the words sent her into cold chills. Yet she took no action to seek outside help.

Up to this point, all the members of the household had been taken in by the deception of Sarah Haviland and Dr. Daniel Baker. What foiled their plan was the innocence of little Phebe. She went for a walk on Saturday morning. Typically, she was seen walking with her three other siblings, but this time she was alone.

Elijah Clapp in front of his carriage shop, circa 1865. *Willard Library Archives.*

Just north along Jefferson Avenue was the carriage factory owned by Elijah Clapp. He had been working in his shop that Saturday morning, December 16, and saw Phebe walking alone. He called out, asking her where her brothers and little sister were. Sad, she replied that they had died.

Shocked by this news, Elijah walked over to the Haviland shanty, where he knew the children lived. He inquired why the children were not out playing. He was told of their death, confirming what Phebe had told him, and brought into the home and shown the three bodies lying on the floor under a sheet. Before entering the home, he witnessed Dr. Baker digging a hole near a shed.

Elijah could not believe what he was hearing and seeing. He left swiftly to notify the constable. When the constable arrived on the scene, he summoned the coroner. A coroner's inquiry was immediately established. The coroner selected a handful of men in the town as an impromptu jury to investigate. The members of the household were all questioned about the children's deaths, including Sarah and Dr. Baker.

The lack of emotion from Sarah at the loss of her three children was perplexing to those who did the initial interviews. Myron Joy, a jury member, said he spoke with Sarah. When questioned about the dead children, she simply stated their names, saying they were her children.

When Myron arrived, Sarah was lying on the lounge, appearing to be an invalid. She stated she had not had much rest and was fatigued. When asked further questions, she began crying and saying, "I have a lot of troubles and do not know why you should come to my home and make further trouble!"

Myron Joy's initial impression was that Sarah was a frail woman in sorrow for her children.

The coroner, however, was suspicious of both Sarah and Dr. Baker. He ordered the bodies to be taken into town. The children's remains were examined by medical doctors, as there was no sign of scrofula. When they were autopsied, the coroner ordered that the stomachs of the three children be placed in jars and sent to the University of Michigan in Ann Arbor by courier for examination in the chemical lab.

The professor at the lab in Ann Arbor was able to test samples of the tissue in each of the stomachs. With certainty, he identified high concentrations of arsenic. When the results were returned a week later, Sarah Haviland was confronted with the results. Facing the evidence, she voluntarily confessed to the crimes.

Sarah wrote a written confession in which she detailed her arrival in Battle Creek the prior spring. She claimed her drunken husband had driven her out-of-doors after dark because she believed in Spiritualism. She hoped lawyers would help her get property in the divorce, but they ultimately did not. Dr. Baker had assisted her to survive with the children.

She claimed that as the children grew older, she saw their father in them. She worried they would transgress the laws of the land. She feared sending them to live with their father; they would follow in his footsteps, becoming thieves and drunkards. She also saw a worse fate if Libbie lived with him.

Thus it was better to send them to the spirit world.

She omitted that Arthur, in this logic, was the son of Ira Haviland, not John Leonard. Unless, of course, she had begun seeing John while still married to Ira, in a lovers' tryst? If so, isn't it curious that Ira died when he did?

In her confession, she wrote: "I feel that what I have done is to be settled between me and my God and the spirit world."

She then detailed how the Monday prior she had gone into town to get the ingredients of sulphur, cream of tartar and arsenic and mixed them with molasses. She also claimed that no one in the house knew there was arsenic in the mixture.

She further made claims about the three children, now dead. She said she was forced to have them against her consent but tried to bring them up as well as she knew how. She claimed no one had offered her an inducement or threatened her in any manner in her confession. She claimed that Dr. Baker had been like a father to her and her children. Her confession stated she poisoned the children of her own volition and no one else was involved.

Despite her attempts at exonerating Baker, the police were not convinced. They had caught him digging the holes and making wooden boxes for the dead children. During their investigation before the lab results had returned, they had gathered witness testimony that indicated he had full knowledge of the crimes before they happened. He had even traveled to Harmonia before learning of Libbie's death with Hattie Hannis, where he had discussed with her his plans to bury the children. This convinced them of his complicity.

Additionally, when the coroner interviewed him on the evening of Saturday, December 16, and on Sunday, December 17, they asked him about the holes he had been digging. He hesitated and then finally blurted out to the coroner: "I do not see what that has to do with the case!"

Further, in Baker's voluntary statement, which was written down by the coroner, he gave his testimony slowly. When Baker was asked about his knowledge of the children's deaths, the coroner described his response:

"Sometimes after getting a sentence nearly done, he would go back and change his wording, evidently changing his meaning."

Baker signed his statement after several edits. He maintained he had no part in what Sarah had done.

Despite his claim of not having any knowledge of the crimes, he was taken into custody. While he was in custody, he spoke to the constable, who pointed out to him that it was a peculiar, singular circumstance that all the children died. Baker responded: "I was not at all disappointed. It was no more than I expected, they were so badly diseased."

# THE TRIAL

The trial was held the following May, and both Daniel Baker and Sarah Haviland were charged with murder. All the people heretofore mentioned in this story testified about the events surrounding these two prior to the death of the children. The coroner and coroner's jury also testified to their examination of both defendants when they arrived on the scene and the following days as described.

Professor Douglas from the Chemistry Department at the University of Michigan confirmed on the witness stand the discovery of up to 8 grams of arsenic found in Arthur's stomach. To place this in context, 140 milligrams (or .145 grams) would be potentially lethal to an average-sized adult. A child or elderly person would have a much lower threshold. He found similar quantities in the other two children.

Frederick Wingate testified for the defense that he had seen Sarah Haviland in June and she was distraught. She claimed the children's father, John Leonard, had come for the children, and she had no one to protect her.

Hattie Hannis and Lizzie Merritt also testified that Sarah had expressed concerns that John Leonard would come and take the children away from her on different occasions.

Witnesses for the defense testified to seeing John Leonard lingering around outside the jail after Sarah was arrested. One reported that he hung on a fence outside when Sarah was brought out to be taken to the courthouse. He called out to her, "How are you, Mrs. Baker?" Sarah's response was to swoon, claiming she was faint and weak, then requested help with walking.

Her attorneys attempted to mount a defense that Sarah was insane and therefore not guilty of being responsible for committing the murders. The effort was intended to sway the jury to give her a lesser sentence of manslaughter, a common legal tactic. Their defense was her actions were a result of being driven to insanity by her ex-husband, John Leonard.

The prosecution countered with the testimony from several neighboring farmers from Washtenaw County. All maintained that John and Sarah had seemed to get along until she had suddenly moved out with the children. Many also testified that Sarah was never known to swoon, as she had been displaying in court, but had always been of decisive and strong character.

A farmer named Peter Dresser had also known Sarah in Augusta Township. He once attended a circle where Sarah claimed to be influenced by the spirit of a Catholic priest. He later realized she did this because she knew Dresser was there and in the habit of attending that church.

During the trial, Sarah made an effort to present herself as insane. In addition to the swooning and having what was described as "spasms" in the courtroom, she engaged in similar behavior in her cell.

She took off her dress and placed it over the window once, telling the guards that her ex-husband, John Leonard, had been taunting her through there. She also proclaimed to another guard that Libbie had come to her in a dream and was very joyful, wearing a silver band on her waist and an ornament on her head.

Sheriff Houston stated that when he went to check on her, as soon as he placed the key in the lock, she would start acting up. She would shout, "Don't come in," and he found her standing with a large poker in her hand, repeating over and over that she would "split his brains out!"

Despite all of this, he was not convinced. He believed it was all an act, and he told her so.

He testified that after this, Sarah spent a lot of her time in her cell writing letters, and when not doing so, she was asking for books to read.

The surviving children of Sarah Haviland were also brought to testify.

Phebe Haviland, aged eleven, described life in the shanty. She relayed seeing Lizzie Merritt and Hattie Hannis both sitting on the lounge with Dr. Baker more than once. She also explained she saw both of them sitting on his lap at times, but mostly Hattie. She did not witness them doing anything but sitting there. She also described how Hattie would get on Baker's shoulders and grab a beam that was near the ceiling, then hang from it. Sometimes Baker would hold her stomach. She also recounted how Libbie was crying out near the end like someone was hurting her.

Jane Haviland, aged thirteen, who by the time of the trial was living with a family in Ypsilanti, explained how she was at the shanty when Libbie died. She had been there the Sunday before and saw the three children playing as normal. When she arrived the next time, they were sick, and her mother said they had scrofula.

She recounted how when Libbie died, her mother did not say anything. She asked her why she had not gotten a doctor, and Sarah replied, "Baker was a doctor." Her mother then sent her away that evening, stating that she was afraid that Jane would "lose her place." She was not present the next day when John and Arthur died.

William Haviland, aged sixteen, had arrived back in town from New York early in the morning the day Libbie died. He made his way to the shanty. He had rapped at the door for quite some time before Baker came to let him in. Inside, the three children were lying on the floor. They did not get up to greet him. His mother awoke and came out of her room ten minutes later. He was told the children were sick, and he did not see anyone give them breakfast.

William left to go have breakfast in town, and when he returned, he was present when Libbie died. Sarah was holding her in her lap. He later returned to town. While there, he heard about John's death from his sister Jane when visiting her at the hotel. He stated he was sleeping in the bedroom later that evening when Arthur died and heard about it after he awoke from his mother. He mentioned that he heard the children yell and scream many times while there.

Other witnesses emerged from Harmonia, reporting that Dr. Baker in his visits had alluded that the children would soon die and they had been "drawing on him long enough."

## Convicted

The jury ultimately issued a verdict of guilty of murder on three counts for both Sarah Haviland and Dr. Daniel Baker. They both were sentenced to life in prison. Dr. Baker was sent to solitary confinement in Lansing and died two years later.

Sarah was sent to the Michigan State Prison in Jackson in 1866. She was incarcerated at a time when men and women were held in the same facility on North Mechanic Street. The Detroit House of Corrections, a women's prison, had been built in 1861, but the female inmates from Jackson did not get transferred there until 1867. At that time seven women remained behind in solitary confinement and were eventually sent to Detroit in 1877—everyone, except Sarah Haviland.

Sarah Haviland in the Jackson Prison yard with the warden's children, circa 1870. *Courtesy of Jackson District Library.*

Sarah had been retained as a domestic worker taking care of the warden's house and family. She was so embraced by her employers that they affectionately had taken to calling her Aunt Sarah. She worked for the wardens at Jackson Prison for almost thirty years. There is a painting of her taking care of the warden's children in the yard that hung in the office at the prison for years.

She was considered so trustworthy, she earned the honor of being able to occasionally go shopping in town. She was driven by a convict in the prison carriage and never attempted escape. She was said to have actually thwarted two escapes by sounding the alarm during her time in Jackson Prison.

She presented herself as being very religious, professing to have read every book in the prison library. Oddly enough, the 1880 census taken at the Michigan State Prison lists her as not being able to read or write.

## PARDONED

Sarah petitioned Governor Edwin B. Winans for her release in December 1891 and was denied. However, she would petition again, this time to Governor

John Treadway Rich at the end of his term in 1896. Her petitioners included Warden William Chamberlain, ex-wardens George N. Davis, H.F. Hatch and William Humphrey and fifty-year prison chaplain George H. Hickox.

Governor Rich signed the petition before his departure from office, commuting her sentence. This action made national news in papers across the country. Some praised the decision, and others more familiar with the case condemned it as an injustice.

The stories in national papers all seemed to carry the same theme, that she "committed the crime under the influence of Dr. Baker's stronger mind" and she was beloved and trusted by the officials of the prison as no prisoner had been before. They also said she had a daughter in Ontario who had agreed to provide her with a home and was anxious to do so.

Jane had died years before her mother's petition in 1896. Phebe, by then, was said to have just moved to Ontario, according to the Jackson newspaper.

After her release, Sarah did not live with Phebe. Sarah must have communicated with Phebe in order for her to know that she was moving to Ontario. Following her release from prison, Sarah lived in a rooming house in Detroit until her death in 1906.

There was a compelling letter to the editor written on June 15, 1895, sent to a Jackson newspaper during the time when Sarah was apparently making her appeal for release. There had been favorable press calling her Aunt Sarah Haviland by officials at the prison.

The author of this letter did not sign it. The writer knew Sarah from her time in Washtenaw County, and it painted quite a different view of Sarah than the official story in the papers.

The letter stated:

> It seems very strange to hear so much praise going the rounds of the papers about, as they call her, Aunt Sarah Haviland. God forbid that I should ever entitle or call her by that endearing name. I was brought up in the neighborhood where she lived....
>
> Why do those in trust, or those that have in, trust over murderers, seem to pity a mother, who for the sake of a man's advice would murder those three innocent little ones? Could I lead you back 30 years—those who seem to honor that woman, called a mother—to the Ypsilanti old Quaker Meeting house, 7½ miles south of that city, and on a cold gloomy day go inside the little old church, and see weeping eyes over those two little innocent ones, all bloated and of a waxen hue, in two little caskets side by side, lying in death's cold embrace.

*One, little Libbie; I think the other was Johnnie. I shall never forget the gloom that came over me as they were about going to the cemetery with those two, the word came "Do not bury them. There will be another here tomorrow morning." And those little bodies, laid all alone in the old church through the dreary night. Now, look at that woman and release her? Do our laws become void because we have some sympathy? God forbid. We cry for justice and not sympathy. Oh, she has been so good. Allowed privileges against justice. So good, as many are good, because they dare not be any other way.*

The writer then poses this question upon closing: "Why not call back Dr. Baker and liberate him?"

Clearly, the writer of this letter believed that Sarah was manipulating officials and politicians to get her appeal. Apparently, at the time, no one was doing anything to verify what she was claiming. Most of the claims in this letter bore out as facts in the trial transcripts.

Instead, articles claimed she committed the crimes under hypnosis.

An article in the *Jackson Citizen* in 1896 noted, "When the female convicts were removed to Detroit several years ago, she was working in the warden's house and was permitted to remain, and has performed the household work for each succeeding warden's family."

Despite the claims that Sarah made to officials to secure a pardon, there was no mention at all during her trial that she was manipulated by Dr. Baker. In fact, her defense was that John Leonard was to blame for her actions.

Sarah and Dr. Baker made the plan to eliminate the children and then go off and live their vision of a better life together. Baker dug the graves, but Sarah willingly administered the poison to the children. Her story changed with the opportunity to harness the power of sympathy to benefit her cause.

In her own written confession, she exonerated Dr. Baker. One could claim that she did so under his influence, but it is quite convenient for her to have championed this new claim of manipulation years later. Why not? Baker was dead, and dead men tell no tales.

All of the gruesome details of her crimes were overlooked and disregarded in later reviews of her case. A thorough examination of the trial transcripts, however, paints quite a different picture of Sarah Haviland. She was a talented and skilled manipulator, as is clearly demonstrated in how she convinced even those living in her own household that there was nothing suspicious about her children getting sick and dying.

She came close to getting away with it too, had it not been for one suspicious blacksmith named Elijah Clapp who decided to alert the constable. It is likely Baker would have buried the children, and they would have left town before anyone discovered anything was wrong.

Had the coroner not been suspicious enough to have the children's stomachs tested for poison, she quite possibly would have manipulated her way out of being charged with a crime.

Further proof of this is that when Sarah was sent to Jackson in 1866, she was almost exclusively the only woman in the entire prison. The population of Michigan in 1860 was just under 750,000, with approximately 85 to 100 inmates in the Jackson prison. When released, she was the second-oldest inmate, and her prison number was 20.

The Victorian era was a time when men, despite hard evidence of a crime, had a difficult time believing women were capable of murder. Is it any wonder that a manipulator like Sarah succeeded with a convincing story of her being the victim of a man who hypnotized her into committing murder? She convincingly augmented her story with years of good behavior, but the truth is, she heartlessly murdered three innocent children.

Alban Cemetery. *Author's collection.*

# AFTERMATH

The three deceased Haviland children—Arthur, John and Mary Elizabeth "Libbie"—were buried in Alban Cemetery in Washtenaw County in 1866. The original Alban Cemetery location flooded, and caskets were moved in 1886 to a new location, which became the New Alban Cemetery. There are no longer any markers.

Regarding the three surviving children, twenty-year-old William Haviland was working for Silas Whitmore, a produce dealer in Washtenaw County, as a domestic worker in 1870. It was indicated in the census that he could not read or write. He later changed his name to Heaviland, either by intention or by merely someone else misinterpreting the spelling of his own name for him. He married a Canadian, Eva Mosser, in 1893 in Belding, Michigan. At that time, William was listed as being in manufacturing, and his new wife, Eva, was a silk weaver.

That marriage would last only one year, and he married again to an English immigrant named Annie Bell in 1894. At the time of his second marriage, he was listed as a machinist. They had moved to the Grand Rapids area. What became of him after that is unknown.

Jane married Robert Kircher, an Englishman who was a farmer in Washtenaw County. She passed away around 1882 and is buried in Washtenaw County.

Phebe married twice. She passed away in October 1910 in Lansing, Michigan, at the age of fifty-six, listed as a widowed housekeeper on her death certificate. At the time of her death, her last name was listed as Baker.

# 7
# DARK SECRET IN A SANDBANK (1875)

*Secrets, silent, stony sit in the dark palaces of both our hearts:*
*secrets weary of their tyranny: tyrants willing to be dethroned.*
—*James Joyce*

In 1875, the houses that are on both sides of Rittenhouse Avenue in Battle Creek today were just beginning to be built. The section of the road between Caroline Street and South Washington had only one home standing along the south side of the street. That was the home of John Meachem, a local surveyor who had donated the land on this block, known as Meachem's Addition.

On either side of his home there were four to five undeveloped lots, and across the street there was a row of five vacant lots and a small public park that he had donated to the city as well. The park still exists today as Prospect Park.

## GRISLY DISCOVERY

It was a Monday afternoon, about four o'clock, on September 27 of that year, when workmen shoveling dirt in a sandbank in one of the vacant lots across from Meachem's house made a grisly discovery that brought an abrupt end to their workday. Buried eight inches deep in the sandy embankment was the body of a two-week-old girl with clothes on, without a box or coffin.

A coroner's jury was empaneled by Justice T.W. Hall within a few hours to hold a formal inquiry into the matter. The inquest was adjourned until nine o'clock the next morning, when Dr. Simeon French conducted a postmortem examination of the remains. In the doctor's opinion, it was a child that had been alive previous to its burial, an estimated six to ten days before the discovery. The little girl died from suffocation, or possibly strangulation, according to the findings of Dr. French.

He estimated the body had been in ground five to six days and speculated that whoever killed the child had intended to leave it at someone's door but for some reason had changed their mind and buried it instead. He made this conclusion because the child was fully dressed as infants usually are as the weather gets cooler.

# Investigation

The inquest was not able to discover any immediate clues to the identity of the child, much less who had committed the crime that first week. In fact, it would not be until late November that they would learn the identity of the child's mother: Anna Owens, a domestic worker, who resided in Coldwater, Michigan. How they came to discover her identity is not clear, but the investigation led the authorities to Owens.

Three weeks following this discovery, both Anna and her fiancé, Austin Smith, a resident of Battle Creek and a blacksmith by trade, were charged with the murder of the infant. The details of the events leading up to the child's death would slowly be revealed as the trial moved forward in the courts.

For about a year and a half prior to the incident, Anna Owens and Austin Smith had been living in what was described in the newspapers as "improper intimacy." In the Victorian era, this kind of behavior was considered not only improper but there were potential punitive statutes that could sometimes be enforced by the courts if discovered as well.

Austin Smith had been arrested in Battle Creek previously and charged with "bastardy" when another girl, Adaline Toland, in the city pressed a case against him. He was still under bonds with the court for child support for that incident when he was arrested in this case. The outcome of the prior case compelled Austin to begin using the alias Austin Joyce in his business dealings, because he had been accused of fathering an illegitimate child.

On the morning of December 13, Owens and Smith were brought before Judge Hall on the charge of murder, and both waived further examination, entering a plea of not guilty, and a trial was scheduled for the next term in the spring.

Austin was taken to jail in Marshall, Michigan. Anna was remanded to the care of the sheriff in Battle Creek and retained at the courthouse. While in his care, she was overtaken with anxiety and transferred to the State Insane Asylum in Kalamazoo on Friday, December 21. It was reported later that Smith tried to pretend that he was also insane while in jail in Marshall. The newspapers claimed it was a ruse to facilitate an escape from the fate that awaited him.

# The Trial

The trial was held in March 1876. It was revealed that eighteen-year-old Anna had moved to Coldwater in August and begun work as a domestic worker for a man named Abbott. She represented herself as being married when seeking work from Mr. Abbott and was in fact eight months pregnant. She had left Battle Creek to conceal her pregnancy from her parents.

She gave birth around the first of September and sent word to Austin Smith in Battle Creek. A few weeks later, Smith traveled to Coldwater in an open buggy he had borrowed to take her back to Battle Creek.

It was September 19 when he arrived, and he loaded up Anna and the newborn into the buggy. They began their journey back on the cold early autumn evening. On the way back, it began to rain, and Anna told Austin she was beginning to get sick. Austin wrapped Anna and the infant in blankets, covered them both with a buffalo robe and continued their journey.

When they neared Battle Creek, they discovered the infant was dead. Underneath the heavy load of blankets, the child had suffocated. Anna claimed later that she was terrified when making the discovery and had exclaimed to Austin, "My God! What shall we do?"

Austin, she stated, had replied: "You go to your aunt's, and I will do the best I can."

Austin then drove Anna over to her aunt's house and left her there for the night. He then took the body of the child and left it bundled up in an outhouse at his own mother's house while he returned the horse and buggy.

He later returned to the outhouse and, under the cover of the rainy night, buried it in the sandbank along Rittenhouse. It was just down the street from his mother's house near the park. He later claimed he had intended to return at a future date and give it a proper burial, but he had waited too long and the body had already been discovered.

When the baby was traced back to both himself and Anna, Austin told the police that the child was alive when they returned to Battle Creek and that he had given it to a man named John Quailing who was moving to Montcalm County. He claimed to not know what had happened to it after that.

Likely this was a story that Anna and he created after the body was discovered, to place blame on an unknown third party. He was reported to have also told Anna to tell her friends that she had given the child to Austin and he had given it away.

The police investigating the incident were not persuaded by Smith's story. They found inconsistencies between Anna and Austin's stories and instead took his claim as an admission of guilt to having murdered the child. His failed attempt at a cover story led to a charge of murder for not only himself but also Anna.

During the trial, the prosecution presented the case that the evidence tended to show that Smith had seduced the girl Anna Owens and was the father of the child, and the child was born out of wedlock in Coldwater. They also presented that Owens's parents knew nothing of the birth of the child, that Smith and Owens on the night of the murder rode from Coldwater to Battle Creek in a buggy and the child was just two weeks old. On arriving in Battle Creek after nightfall, Smith took the child from the mother, which was the last time it was seen until found buried in the sandbank.

The defense claimed that the child was dead when Smith took it from its mother. Anna was not permitted to testify by the judge in Austin's defense, and his prior reputation with the bastardy conviction did not strengthen his position. Additionally, Dr. French's medical testimony of how he believed the child was smothered or strangled was given strong consideration.

The jury, after being out in deliberation for only about two hours, found him guilty of murder in the first degree. Austin Smith was sentenced to solitary confinement at hard labor for life in the state prison on March 23, 1876.

## Aftermath

The trial for Anna was postponed to the following term. The evidence of her complicity in the murder was considered slight, and she was allowed to make bail until her trial. The charges against her would ultimately be dismissed.

Austin Smith's headstone at Oak Hill Cemetery, Battle Creek, Michigan. *Author's collection.*

A year later, on February 10, 1877, Austin Smith was granted a new trial in an appeal considered by Judge Philip Taylor Van Zile of the Calhoun County Circuit Court. In the new trial, this time Anna Owens was allowed to testify.

She made the case that the child had died in their journey that night between Coldwater and Battle Creek. She stated on the witness stand that rather than parade their disgrace for having been so negligent with the care of the newborn, the dead infant was buried in the sand by the roadside.

Anna's testimony must have been quite convincing during the weeklong trial. After a twenty-four-hour deliberation, the jury returned with a verdict of not guilty and Austin was released.

Before leaving the courtroom, Austin Smith and Anna Owens asked the presiding judge if he would marry them right there on the spot, and the judge obliged. They were married in the presence of the court.

One year later, on May 24, 1878, Austin Smith passed away in the arms of his mother. His last request was to send a thank-you to his defense attorney, Leonidas Dibble, to reassure him that he was entirely innocent of murdering the child, the crime for which he was acquitted. He died of consumption, the Victorian-era name for tuberculosis. He is buried in Oak Hill Cemetery in Battle Creek.

# 8
# THE DEATH OF A GIANT
# (1875)

*A party of roughs were gambling in Hodge's saloon, which is one of the worst*
*sink-holes in the county, when a dispute arose.*
—Marshall Statesman, *October 6, 1875*

In 1875, on the corner of Main and Jefferson Streets in Battle Creek, there stood the New Chicago Clothing House owned by J.M. Jacobs. Jacobs's store offered clothing, specializing in furs, hats, caps, scarfs, gloves, coats, neckties, collars and suspenders in regular advertisements in the newspapers of the time. The store, although primarily a men's clothing store, also carried children's clothing and linens for the home. Over the years, this store also bore the name of the New York Clothing Store and the Boston Clothing Store.

In the basement of this store, there existed a saloon owned by Samuel Hodges. It was described as one of the worst sinkholes in the county. Inside were two rooms, one where billiards was played, which also included dining tables, and the other for playing cards. Men from all over the area would venture down to the saloon during the daytime and evening to play cards or billiards, smoke cigars, eat food and enjoy some drinks.

## THE CARD GAME

Shortly after one o'clock in the afternoon on Friday, October 1, 1875, a group of four men were playing cards—which of course included gambling. At the

The New York Clothing Store, Battle Creek, Michigan, circa 1880. *Kurt Thornton Collection.*

table were Emory Nye, Thomas Betts, John Chambers and Robert Farrell. Thomas Betts was the brother-in-law of Emory Nye. The two had ridden into town together in a carriage, which was parked across the street from the saloon. Both Nye and Betts were known in the community for their checkered past.

John Chambers, the oldest man at the table at sixty, was a veteran of the Civil War. Sitting next to John was Robert Farrell, an Irish tailor who had lived in Battle Creek since the spring of 1864.

In the adjoining room, Theron Mason and Robert Molyneaux were having a conversation in the billiard room, where they also served food. Robert had arrived in the saloon for the purpose of having lunch and had just ordered his meal.

Theron had been a lieutenant in the Civil War and was originally from Bellevue, but he had moved to Battle Creek at the close of the war.

Robert Molyneaux, aged thirty-six, was a giant of a man and also a Civil War veteran who had been wounded in action in 1863 serving with Company C, Second Michigan Infantry. An Irishman, he lived in Johnstown Township and was known for his strength and skills as a fighter.

He was also married to his wife, Ellen, and the father of five children, three sons and two daughters.

While Robert and Theron were waiting for the food, they walked over to the doorway of the card room to watch the game in progress.

The men around the table were playing for beer on this early afternoon. While Robert and Theron watched, Chambers was beaten in the game, losing his hand and required to pay for that round of beer. He settled what he claimed he owed and made it known he no longer wished to continue playing. With that, he stood up and began to move away from the table.

Emory Nye, however, was not willing to accept his departure or the amount of his payment. He demanded more money. He also insisted that Chambers sit back down and continue to play. Chambers held steadfast in his determination not to play another hand or part with another dime. Nye, however, became insistent, and demanded more boisterously that he do so. The argument became heated, and voices were raised—neither man giving on their position.

Witnesses described that hard words were exchanged between Nye and Chambers, neither backing down on the matter. At that point, Molyneaux stepped in between the two and talked to them, in an effort to get them to cool down.

The two seemed to quiet down, but shortly after, their argument began again. Nye insisted that Chambers pay more money, and Chambers refused to do so. Then Betts stood up next to Nye, and both struck Chambers with their fists in this exchange.

## The Giant Intervenes

Molyneaux interceded again. This time he told Nye not to abuse an old man and that he should leave Chambers alone. At this declaration, Thomas Betts stepped up to confront Molyneaux. Threatening, he demanded to know what Molyneaux had to do with the matter, and what did he want to come of it?

Molyneaux looked at Betts and told him it suited him just fine if something were to come of it, and both men took off their coats. The two men went at each other, and Molyneaux, being the stronger man, punched Betts so hard it threw him bodily off his feet into the corner of the room.

Seeing his brother-in-law tossed aside by the larger man, Nye entered the fray and charged him. Molyneaux struck Nye hard, tossing him across the room as well, landing him on his back, also in the corner.

Downtown Battle Creek, Michigan, circa 1880. *Kurt Thornton Collection.*

Betts, having regained his footing, began to charge Molyneaux again, but Robert Farrell checked him, preventing him from continuing the fight. While Molyneaux was facing Betts in a stare down, Nye got to his feet. He covertly pulled a knife out of his coat and stabbed Molyneaux in the stomach before swiftly darting up the stairs and out the front door of the saloon.

Molyneaux instantly clutched his bowels and exclaimed that he had been cut. He passed through the billiard room and up the stairs into the street. He stumbled once at the top of the stairs, righted himself, uttered a cry for help and then collapsed in the street. Molyneaux lost consciousness and died in the intersection from his wound within minutes.

Meanwhile, Nye had made it to his carriage and was quickly taking off down the street with the horse at a gallop. Betts, seeing that he was being left behind, ran up and out of the saloon. With a glance at Molyneaux lying in the street, he sprinted after the carriage.

As he saw the two men run from the saloon and also witnessed Molyneaux's collapse in the street, a police officer named Alexander Briggs gave foot pursuit. Nye stopped the carriage about three blocks down the street, only long enough to allow Betts to climb aboard, and then the two set the horse off again at a fast pace. Officer Briggs later arrested both of them at Nye's residence and escorted them to the office of Justice Hall downtown.

# Arrested

The two were taken before Judge Hall, and he ordered them placed on an express train to Marshall to be detained pending an inquiry and charges. The body of Robert Molyneaux was carried to the Michigan Tribune building nearby. Examination by the coroner would determine the wound was caused by a blade or some other sharp pointed cutting instrument. The blade had penetrated through his stomach and protruded out of his backbone.

Witnesses came forward to testify to the events that happened that day in the saloon. Others also testified to seeing Betts and Nye bury the murder weapon in their backyard, which was later excavated and presented at trial.

Emory Nye's defense initially tried to deny the stabbing, but when the knife and witness testimony was presented, they switched their arguments to one of self-defense. The prosecution brought a wave of testimony that the deceased was a peaceable man. The jury agreed and brought a decision of guilty of murder in the first degree.

Emory Nye, having been convicted of murder, erupted and told the judge that he did not care if he was given forty years in prison. He exclaimed that human life was held in light esteem to him and that this was not the first time he had done such a thing. The judge, making the determination that Nye was a man devoid of all moral character, who had no care for the rights or souls of others, sentenced him to life in prison.

Witnesses at the trial described Nye as being as dead as the Frankenstein monster, with no countenance or emotion when the awful details of his act were revealed in court. Nye was only twenty-four years old, and it was alleged at the trial that he had been raised in a house of prostitution. His mother, present at the trial, was said to have been the madam of six to eight of these institutions in the county at the time of the trial.

Ellen Molyneaux, Robert's wife, openly wept in the courtroom. The citizens of Marshall who were present during the trial were outraged at Nye's oration within the courtroom, and the papers claimed they rejoiced knowing this evil man was going to be expelled from the county.

The sheriff took Nye to Jackson Prison within a few days, and he remained there for a year while his attorneys filed an appeal. The case was taken to the Michigan Supreme Court, and a new trial was granted on the point that malice was not proven. At the second trial in 1876, he was convicted of manslaughter and sentenced to the penitentiary for twenty-five years.

# Aftermath

Betts was also charged as an accessory, and a trial was held in Marshall in December. He appears to have been released, as in February 1876, he was arrested again, this time for burglary in Battle Creek. While waiting for his trial in that case, he attempted to escape the jail and was caught. In an effort to exonerate another inmate, he claimed it was entirely his own plan and was solely responsible for the escape attempt.

He had attempted a similar testimony in the Molyneaux murder case, in an effort to exonerate Nye by claiming it was his responsibility for starting the fight with Robert. The judge and the jury, with the help of the prosecution, gave no weight to this testimony, as it was clear from all the witnesses it was Nye who committed the murder.

Robert Molyneaux was buried in Young's Cemetery off Goguac Road a few days following his murder.

Ellen Molyneaux sued the saloon owner, Samuel Hodges, for damages in the loss of her husband in 1876. The case settled for $10,000, a value of around $277,000 today. She also applied for Robert's widow pension in 1890 for his service in the Civil War. She moved away from Michigan with her children back to Maryland, where she was raised, and later settled in Washington, D.C. Ellen never remarried, and she passed away in 1896 from pneumonia, followed by a bout with typhoid fever at the age of fifty-six.

John Chambers, the man whom Molyneaux was protecting, lived to the age of seventy-five and passed away in 1891. He is buried at Reese Cemetery in Springfield, Michigan.

Robert Farrell, the Irish tailor, passed away in 1884 and is buried at Mt. Olivet Cemetery in Battle Creek.

In 1903, at the age of sixty, Lieutenant Theron Mason passed away at Nichols Hospital in Battle Creek, where he had been admitted for a heart condition and contracted pneumonia. He is buried at Oak Hill Cemetery in Battle Creek, and today his tombstone is almost completely consumed by a tree that was planted next to his grave at the time of his death.

An interesting story ran in the *Hillsdale Standard* on March 7, 1876. It described a Kalamazoo man showing up in Murphy's Saloon in Battle Creek and remarking aloud, "It is a good thing that Bob Molyneaux, who was killed by Emory Nye, was out of the way." At this, a young man from the country jumped up, and when he got through with that stranger, he was described as a well-pounded individual.

Those in the saloon who watched the encounter all shouted "Good!"

It was later discovered the Kalamazoo "stranger" was one of Emory Nye's brothers.

# 9

# THE THOMAS LILLEY
# CASE (1876)

*When Lilley got to town—Dowagiac—he found Krieger there considerably
under the influence of liquor, and he "went for" Lilley in a very abusive manner,
threatening to knock the hell out of him.*
—St. Joseph Herald Press, *January 18, 1879*

Saturday, November 11, 1876, was a day that would indelibly haunt the memory of Thomas Lilley. He had spent the prior three months recovering from an illness. Before this ailment, he weighed 150 pounds and had a lot of strength and energy. After he had gotten through the troublesome three months, his health was finally on the mend again. Although considerably weaker and now weighing just 115 pounds, he was beginning to regain his energy. He was thirty-two years old and was living on his farm with his wife, Nancy, who was twenty-six, and his seven-year-old daughter, Sara.

## CHARLES KRIEGER

While Lilley was recovering, he hired some additional laborers to work around the farm. One of these men was twenty-five-year-old Charles Krieger from Bainbridge, in Berrien County.

Charles rented a room in the house while he worked on the farm. Despite his recent troubles with his health, Lilley, who was just thirty-two years old, was a fairly wealthy farmer for his time. He owned a four-hundred-acre farm that straddled two townships in Cass County, just south of Dowagiac. He was able to pay wages during the time when he could not work, which kept his farm in production during the harvest.

On that Saturday in November, the work had been completed for the season. The laborers approached him for their pay. During Charles's time working at the Lilley farm, he had borrowed a powder flask and a slouch pouch and not returned these as promised. In the 1800s, a powder flask was a container used to carry gunpowder, an essential piece of equipment to accompany a muzzle-loading gun when hunting. A slouch pouch was usually a bag to carry things in, but in this case, it could also have been referring to a bullet bag that went along with the powder flask.

When it came time for Thomas Lilley to settle with Charles on his wages, he withheld funds in the amount of $3.25 for the cost of the unreturned powder flask and pouch from his final payment. He told Charles that when he returned the items or replaced them, he would disburse to him the sum he had retained.

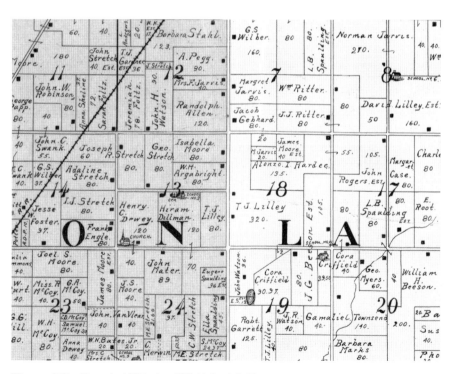

Thomas Lilley Farm in 1897 atlas. *U.S. National Archives.*

Charles said nothing during this exchange and took his money. Thomas offered Charles a ride into town, as he was leaving in his wagon within the hour to go into Dowagiac. Instead, Charles declined and headed into town alone on foot.

# CONFRONTATION

Later that day, when Thomas Lilley arrived in town, Krieger came out of a saloon very intoxicated and, seeing him, swiftly approached. He began shouting abusive curses, threatening to knock the hell out of him. Lilley retreated down the street to Marshal Hannon's office to avoid Krieger. The marshal advised Lilley to just leave town and come back and do his business another day. Agreeing with the marshal, he left town.

After Lilley left Dowagiac, Charles Krieger decided to hire a team of horses to go back to Lilley's farm under the premise of "collecting his clothes." He took along with him a friend named Jacob Cooke, who had also been employed by Lilley. The man he hired the horse and wagon from sent his son along to help manage the horses.

After arriving at the Lilley farm, Charles Krieger collected his clothes from the house and put them in the wagon. Leaving Cooke and the hired man at the wagon, he went into the backyard of the house in search of Thomas Lilley.

By this time, it was nearly dark, as the sun was low on the horizon. There, still intoxicated, he confronted Lilley, demanding his money, or he was going to "lick him right then and there!"

Charles weighed 175 pounds and was a strong young man. Lilley was a mere 115 pounds and not in good health. Krieger charged Lilley when he refused, and a struggle ensued. Overpowered, Lilley pulled out a knife from his pocket, slashing and stabbing at Krieger randomly, cutting him in several places. One of the stabs landed deep in the flesh of his chest near his heart. Krieger withdrew, with knees buckling, and fell to the ground.

Lilley summoned Cooke and the wagon driver who had arrived with Krieger. At the time, the two men, along with Lilley, thought Krieger was just passed out from the alcohol and overexerting himself. All three loaded him into the wagon to take him to a doctor in Dowagiac to dress his wounds. It was almost entirely dark by this time. Cooke rode in the back of the wagon with Krieger's head in his lap, occasionally tapping his cheek, trying to wake him. About one and a half miles into their return trip, Cooke realized Krieger was dead.

# Tried and Tried Again

The marshal returned later that evening and arrested Thomas Lilley. The trial began on March 6, 1877, in Cassopolis in Judge Coolidge's courtroom in Cass County. Lilley's defense team argued it was self-defense and made their case as such. The trial lasted ten days, and the jury brought a verdict of manslaughter.

The sentence was never enforced, however, as the decision was immediately appealed to the Michigan Supreme Court. Lilley's appeal disagreed with the ruling, citing that the instructions that had been given to the jury by the judge were not included within the law. Judge Coolidge had instructed the jury before going into deliberation: "A person cannot kill another in self-defense without first trying to get away from the assailant, and second without calling assistance from those who may be nearby."

While the case was being appealed, Lilley was released on a $10,000 bond, which was quite large for the time. Some of the press insinuated Lilley was getting favorable treatment because he was wealthy and had influential friends making it possible to do this. However, other papers of the time examined the judge's statements and reported that the case had merit.

The appeal to the Michigan Supreme Court was filed. The legal exception cited the instructions given by the judge to the jury were outside the parameters of the law. After examination, the court sustained the exception. They then ordered a new trial should be held. Lilley's defense team filed a motion to have the new trial moved to Berrien County, on the grounds that Lilley would receive a fair trial, instead of Cass County. The court approved the motion.

The new trial was held in October 1878 in Berrien County, and the state selected Judge Hawes from Kalamazoo to preside. Lilley testified at the new trial that he did not intend to kill Krieger and did not think the wounds were fatal at the time. His attorneys also argued that he helped place Krieger in the wagon. Witnesses to the incident, and earlier in town, all testified that Krieger had been the aggressor.

The trial lasted until January 1879. The new jury agreed with the defense, and Lilley was acquitted. After three long years, the legal case was behind him.

The trouble in Lilley's life, however, was far from over.

In 1907, Thomas Lilley drove his wife and daughter from their home in June, and by September, he was judged by the courts to be insane. He was then committed to the state asylum. He passed away in 1909 at the age of sixty-four and is buried in Riverside Cemetery in Dowagiac, Michigan.

# 10

# THE CROUCH MURDERS (1883)

*The Crouch place had a weary, somber and deserted appearance....*
*The perspective of ragged, gray cornfields, leafless orchards, tumble down barns*
*and the faded weather beaten house, from which the ancient shutters, once painted*
*green, but now broken and unhinged, flapped in the brisk wind. Among all of the*
*residences along this road, this was the least likely to be selected by a stranger as*
*the home of a wealthy man, but it would quickly be pointed out as a fit place for*
*the commission of a terrible deed of violence.*
—Jackson Citizen Patriot, *1883*

Jacob Crouch was one of four brothers who settled in Jackson County, near Spring Arbor, about seven miles from the town of Jackson in 1833. In those days, he was described as an energetic, close-fisted and thrifty farmer. He acquired five hundred acres of land to raise wheat. He married Anne Birch in 1838, and together they had three sons and two daughters. Anne passed away in 1859, and Jacob never remarried.

On the evening of November 21, 1883, at his home, Jacob D. Crouch, now a wealthy seventy-four-year-old farmer; William Henry White, his son-in-law, aged thirty; and his daughter Eunice White, who was nine months pregnant at age thirty-three, sat in the sitting room of their rural country home. With them was their guest Moses Polley, a twenty-three-year-old drover from Pennsylvania visiting Mr. Crouch on business.

Eunice was born in that house and had graduated from St. Mary's College, Notre Dame eighteen years prior, having converted to the Catholic faith prior to her marriage. Henry was born in Scotland and had been a resident of Jackson County since infancy. Moses Polley had previously lived with Jacob Crouch and married Minnie Anson, who also used to live with Jacob. They had moved to Pennsylvania and recently had a child. Moses was back in Spring Arbor to purchase a few cattle for his farm.

The four sat around listening to the prevailing wind and driving rain outside. As the storm continued to build, the skies grew darker. They were enjoying some hot apple cider along with some sliced apples before retiring for the evening.

Also in the home was a sixteen-year-old Black farmhand, George Boles, who was employed by Crouch. He stayed in the only upstairs bedroom. Additionally, Julia Reese, a young girl, lived in the back bedroom of the house near the kitchen and was employed as a domestic worker for Crouch.

# ASSASSINATION

Unbeknownst to four of them, this would be their last night on earth. Sometime between when they retired for the evening and early morning, all four would be shot and found in their beds. None survived to identify their attackers.

During the night, the storm increased in intensity, with violent winds and heavy rain. George Boles testified later that he went to bed at eight o'clock that evening. Before he retired, he heard Moses Polley discussing the cattle purchase with Mr. Crouch.

He recounted how he was awakened in the night by a noise he could not identify, followed by the sound of someone crying out "Oh!" twice, and then noises of someone pounding heavily on the floor below. The storm outside was intense with heavy winds, blowing the window shutters against the house.

George stated he became frightened, thus did not venture down to investigate. Instead, he said, he opened a trunk in his room and climbed inside, sleeping there the rest of the night. In the morning, he awoke early as he usually did around five o'clock. As part of his usual routine, he headed downstairs to make the fire. He called out for Mr. Crouch; hearing no reply, he investigated and made a gruesome discovery. Mr. Crouch, Mr. Polley, Henry and Eunice White all lay in their beds, dead. Blood was everywhere.

Dressed only in a woolen shirt and a pair of pants, Boles ran to a neighboring farm owned by the Clements. He returned with a man who worked there named George Hutchinson. Upon seeing the bodies, Hutchinson instructed

MRS. EUNICE WHITE.

HENRY WHITE.

JACOB CROUCH.

MOSES POLLEY.

Jacob Crouch (taken after deceased), William and Eunice White, Moses Polley, 1883. *From the* Jackson Citizen Patriot.

Boles to run to the nearby farm of Dan Holcomb, another son-in-law of Jacob Crouch, to tell them of the discovery. Initially, on seeing all of the blood, Hutchinson believed the victims all had their throats cut. Bullet wounds would be discovered later.

George Boles returned from the Holcombs' farm with Judd Crouch, aged twenty-four, the youngest son of Jacob Crouch, along with James Foy, a man in the employ of Dan Holcomb.

When Judd Crouch arrived, he went inside the home. Something that would be recalled as odd later by onlookers is that Foy remained outside. Farmers from the area assembled outside the home and began talking among themselves. They chatted about lynching the murderer. It was during this time it was noted that Foy, as one described, "sneaked off like a hound." Neighbors also noted Judd Crouch's seeming absence of emotions in the loss of his father and sister.

# Investigation

Within hours, hundreds of people arrived at the murder scene. Initial speculation was the culprit's intent was robbery. Witnesses who arrived at the scene early that morning reported the house smelled of chloroform.

Sheriff Winney was the first law enforcement present, arriving around nine o'clock. He noted the scene and called for assistance from Chief of Police Burkhart and three other officers, Snyder, Mann and Murray. Dr. William Gibson was called to examine the bodies. Coroner Casey arrived and empaneled six men to serve as a jury of inquiry.

When the officers arrived, there was a crowd of people. Several dozen had already been through the house, gawking and looking for clues. Many amateur sleuths had begun searching the house for evidence, moving furniture and even moving the bodies.

Some of the evidence found included five empty cartridge shells from a .38-caliber revolver in the dirt below a windowsill. There was an impression of a footprint on top of them, which could easily have been from any of the onlookers. Spent bullets were also found inside the home and inside the bedding. Some items were found by the police and others presented to them when they arrived.

There was no indication the officers asserted authority, ordering everyone out of the home during the investigation. Today, we expect crime scenes to be secured and access given only to law enforcement. However, this was the Victorian era. Police often were late on the scene.

The police took what evidence they could find and began the process of interviewing neighbors, trying to find clues to the identity of the killer or killers. It was a slow process.

As this tragedy was investigated, the detectives became persuaded the intent was murder, in addition to robbery. All four victims were shot multiple times. Crouch appeared to have been shot first, followed by Polley. Their bodies were moved and placed on the beds.

Crouch was found lying in his bed, with his face to the wall, arms crossed on his chest and a bullet wound to the back of the head. Polley was found lying in the same position in his room, facing the wall, and also shot in the back of the head. When his body was further examined, more bullet wounds were found in his chest.

The Whites were shot where they slept, as Henry was found with his arm underneath Eunice. One bullet struck his temple; another entered the neck, severing his jugular. This sent sprays of blood over Eunice's face, the bedding and the walls of the room. Eunice was shot four times; two bullet holes were in her right arm above the elbow, one in the chin, one in her left wrist and another through her right breast. The one through her wrist was the same bullet that struck her chin, as if she had been covering her face from the killer.

Polley, described as a "braggadocio," was reported by witnesses who had seen him in town before his arrival at the Crouch farm. He had arrived at Baldwin's Station the prior day. He made some purchases there, exhibiting large rolls of bills in his coat. It was estimated he had about $1,700 with him. He was described as talking freely about purchasing cattle at a saloon and recklessly displaying his wealth to some foreigners who were working on the railroad. Some speculated that he had been followed home by thieves.

It was also believed that Jacob Crouch had $56,000 in his possession. He had recently received some funds from claims he sold at a Texas cattle ranch. Later, a silver watch of Henry White was also reported missing.

Julia Reese awoke to a quiet house and emerged from her room. Not entering the front rooms, she began preparing breakfast in the kitchen, unaware that anything had happened. That was where she was found when the alarmed neighbors arrived. Outraged at her lack of awareness, she was abruptly taken and shown the carnage in the front bedrooms.

Julia told investigators that she never heard anything. She was known to be a sound sleeper, and the room she was staying in was in the very back of the house. With the intense storm, it is plausible she heard nothing. However, when questioned about her movements the night before, she mentioned she always locked the exterior doors. Neighbors quickly pointed out to the police that the doors were never locked. Further examination revealed the locks on the doors were worn and barely latched when the doors were closed.

When questioned by police, Boles described hearing the strange noise and not investigating until morning. He told his story of hiding in the trunk. The room he was staying in was directly over the rooms where the murders took place. In his room, the police examined the trunk, discovering it was half full of books. They made several attempts to see if someone of Boles's size could climb inside the remaining space and close the lid, to no success. Additionally, it was discovered that Boles's brother had been fired by Jacob Crouch a few days before the incident, which cast a suspicion of motive on him.

One can only speculate, but it is highly probable that George Boles knew more about what happened than he was willing to tell. Perhaps he saw the killers or could identify them. He was a young Black teenager among a group of angry white adults. For his own self-preservation, he may have decided to remain silent, lest he become the convenient target. As a result of his silence, he would spend seven weeks in jail.

Julia was arrested as well. The police believed it was impossible for either of them to have slept through the night without hearing the intruders or the shooting. Further, both of their stories left investigators with more questions than answers. Eventually, they were released without charges two months later.

David Easton, Union City postmaster and newspaper editor. *Courtesy of Bobbie Mathis.*

## FOY UNHINGED

A few weeks later, mid-January 1884, two men visiting from Jackson went to the Crouch homestead to look over the scene of the tragedy. They reported later that James Foy appeared and showed them the home like a tour guide. They noted he was somewhat under the influence of liquor. Foy was quite talkative, describing the murders in detail with great minuteness.

Foy told them Jacob Crouch was murdered first and then Moses Polley heard the noise and came to the door. Polley was killed next and then carried back to the bed.

One of the visitors remarked, "One person must have killed them all," and Foy retorted: "No, no; one killed the old man and Polley; there was two in the job; the other killed Eunice and Henry White."

The conversation soon ended, but the detail in which Foy described the murders impressed on the visitors that he knew more about the tragedy than he was telling. They reported their experience to the police.

Police detectives began to follow Foy around, surveilling him. Rumors began to spread that Foy was involved. The story reached the Union City postmaster, Major David J. Easton, who was also the editor of the newspaper.

Easton published a story in the *Union City Register* stating that Foy was involved. Foy had spent some time there as a field laborer before and was known. He eventually saw the article and became angry.

A blacksmith later testified in the trial that Judd Crouch had a similar reaction when seeing the article while visiting his shop.

On Tuesday, February 5, 1884, James Foy began drinking, as was his usual practice. He rambled to others around him that he was being watched by detectives. He told E.H. Howell that he was going to Union City to "fix some things up there," which might detain him for a few days. He showed him a revolver, boasted he had plenty of money and said he knew where he could get more if he ran short.

Foy boarded a train to Union City. On arriving there, he wandered the streets, becoming quite boisterous, decrying Easton and his article. His demonstrations, however, were not considered by police officers or the railroad officials to be anything more than the boastful vagaries of a drunken man. When they approached him, they contented themselves with attempting to quiet him. Once they had a measure of success with this, they left him alone.

Between eleven o'clock and noon, Foy went into the post office and bought some stamps from postmaster Easton. He then made threats to Easton before leaving.

A short while later, a young assistant postmaster, Elmer Shuler, and a friend were seen walking away from the post office. Foy suddenly appeared from hiding under some stairs, holding a gun, when they came around a corner.

He shouted "Halt!" and then fired three shots at Shuler. Foy had been waiting for Easton, misidentifying Elmer for the postmaster. One bullet missed, but the other two found their mark, striking Elmer. One hit his neck about an inch below the ear, just missing his jugular vein. The other struck his cheek.

The pistol Foy had used was a .38 caliber, the same as in the Crouch tragedy. Immediately after the shooting, it was reported that Foy exclaimed, "I have shot the wrong man!" and ran away.

Foy escaped Union City and jumped aboard an outgoing freight train heading east. He was later discovered by a conductor on the approach to Homer and put off the train.

Meanwhile, Elmer Shuler was seriously injured but would ultimately survive the shooting. He was conscious enough to positively identify Foy as the gunman. For many days, however, it was reported his condition was critical.

After being put off the train, Foy walked to Spring Arbor, a distance of thirty miles. At six o'clock Wednesday morning, he arrived at the home of Dan Holcomb, where he boarded. He remained in the house until the afternoon, when officers arrived to arrest him.

It was presumed that Foy saw the officers coming. It was believed he went into the kitchen, placed his pistol against his head and pulled the trigger. He was found dead on the floor when the officers searched the home.

Many would speculate later that Foy was murdered, and the suicide was staged. All that the coroners could confirm was that the gun was fired close to his head, based on powder burns around the entry wound. They disclosed this was consistent with a suicide or a shooter in close proximity.

## The Hunt for Suspects

Detectives, being aware of Foy's involvement and loose tongue, were continuing to investigate to locate other shooters in the Crouch murders. Their top suspects soon became Dan Holcomb, who was also the employer of James Foy, and his son Judd Crouch.

The difficulty the sheriff's department had in this case was the contamination of evidence trampled by gawkers and amateur detectives. Footprints that led into and around the home could have equally been the killer(s) or any of the number of spectators.

A man from Marshall came forward saying he had sold a .38-caliber revolver to Dan Holcomb before the incident. A circumstantial case against both Judd Crouch and Dan Holcomb was slowly assembled. They were ultimately put on trial in October 1884.

A bizarre twist in this story is that on January 2, 1884, Susan Holcomb, the daughter of Jacob Crouch and wife of Daniel Holcomb, was found dead in her bed at home. This was just five to six weeks after the quadruple murder. Her death was later attributed to "fatty degeneration of the heart" by the physicians who examined her body.

Initial reports in the newspaper stated her daughter Edith found her dead in her bedroom, where she had locked the door from the inside. A paper soaked in rat poison was reported to have been found in the dead woman's hand.

Rumors abounded that she did not want to testify against her husband in the upcoming trial and thus took the poison. Without a toxicology investigation, all the doctors could prove was that her heart gave out.

The focus of the trial became not only the review of the four victims murdered on November 21, 1883, but also the shooting of Elmer Schuler and the deaths of James Foy and Susan Holcomb.

Added to the charges was one more incident. On the evening of February 8, when Detective Galen E. Brown was on a road near the Crouch homestead, he was shot.

Brown had once been on the Battle Creek police force before transferring to Jackson. His father had been a physician in Jonesville, Michigan. One witness in the trial that would follow described Brown as too talkative for a detective.

Brown had been on the road near the Crouch homestead. While the officer was surveilling the home, a buggy drove by and a man shot him. Brown would later tell the doctor that he could not identify the shooter, only that he was short and wore a light overcoat and a Scotch cap. The buggy slowed, and a man inquired if his name was Brown. He answered in the affirmative, and then he was shot.

The man left him lying there, continuing down the road. Neighbors who heard the shot went to the relief of Detective Brown, carrying him to a house nearby. He survived.

Dr. Gibson, who examined Brown's wounds, later testified at the trial. He believed that by looking at the angle of the bullet wound, it could have been made from a passing buggy. He surmised from his conversation with him that Brown thought it was Judd Crouch who had shot him.

# The Heirs of Jacob Crouch

The family dynamic is more easily understood when examining the heirs of Jacob Crouch. His two oldest sons, Byron and Dayton, had served in the Civil War. Following the conflict, they settled in Texas.

At the time of Jacob's death, his son Byron Crouch owned a cattle ranch in Texas. Dayton Crouch had died in January 1883. His cause of death in one article inferred he died of typhoid fever, and another reported he was shot to death.

Dayton left a fortune of $50,000 acquired in Mexico to his father, in lieu of other heirs. The estate of Dayton was sold under the direction of Jacob by Bryon, who received $38,000 as a settlement.

Susan Holcomb, his oldest daughter, died in January 1884 from possible suicide. She was the wife of Dan Holcomb.

Judd Crouch, his youngest son, was born twenty-four years prior, just before Jacob Crouch's wife had died. After his wife's death, he entrusted the raising of Judd to his daughter Susan and Daniel Holcomb.

The other daughter was Eunice. Eunice and her husband had been living with Jacob, managing his household for him. Apparently, Jacob and other family had been opposed to her marrying Henry White. Both were killed in the tragedy.

## Property, Perjury and Prosecution

Jacob Crouch's property at the time of his death was a farm of one thousand acres. It was described as some of the richest land in Michigan. He also had an interest in cattle ranches in Texas and held cash on hand. Estimates of his wealth were around $200,000 at the time, over $5 million in today's dollars adjusting for inflation.

His business habits, however, were not prudent. He collected loans, accruing interest from family members and friends, and was reported to have kept money insecurely around the house.

In addition, his relations with his family were not pleasantly maintained. He was not known to be kindly disposed toward any of them. These were principal facts accumulated by authorities during the investigation.

Ultimately, when the trial commenced, Daniel S. Holcomb was charged with the murders of Jacob D. Crouch, Henry White, Eunice White and Moses Polley.

Judd D. Crouch was charged with the same crimes and also the shooting of Detective Galen E. Brown.

Another man, Henry Holcomb, the brother of Daniel, was charged with perjury as a result of the investigation. He had caused the arrest of Joseph Allen, a Canadian, as a suspected murderer of the Crouch family. Henry had alleged that he had tramped about the country with Joseph and that Joseph had confessed many things to him about the case. He turned in Joseph Allen's name to the police, and Allen was subsequently arrested and questioned. After he was thoroughly examined and his alibis checked out, he was acquitted. Henry Holcomb was then arrested and charged with perjury.

Separate trials were demanded, and the trial of Daniel Holcomb was scheduled to begin first.

The prosecution summoned over one hundred witnesses, and the defense also summoned a large number. Initially, the authorities in Jackson County were reluctant to make the appropriations for the trial, as most of the evidence was circumstantial and they doubted whether the trial would result in a conviction.

The post investigation was largely a confusing mess. The coroner postponed the inquest from time to time. Detectives were employed and others volunteered, each seeming to have a different theory. Byron Crouch, when he arrived from Texas, even went so far as to hire the famous Pinkerton Detective Agency out of Chicago and then after some time dismissed them.

Police were suspicious of Daniel Holcomb, whose home was just two miles from the scene. On the night of the murder, Judd Crouch was also living at the house. James Foy, the crazy drunk character who had gone to Union City and shot someone before dying, resided there as well. There were also two other boys, Charles Andrews, aged thirteen, and Fred Lonsberry, aged fifteen.

Police investigating had speculated there could have been anywhere from two to five perpetrators of the crime. A neighbor reported seeing a fresh path through a wheat field that led from Holcomb's farm to the Crouch farm. Completing the list of suspicions was the death of Holcomb's wife earlier in the year.

# The Trial

The trial of Dan Holcomb began on December 4, 1884, more than one year after the murders.

The first witness was Henry J. Crouch, a second cousin of Jacob Crouch, who lived in Liberty Township, near where the tragedy happened. He arrived on the scene of the murder about 1:00 p.m., November 22. He saw Dan Holcomb there, and a bystander told him he had heard that Polley had quite a sum of money in his possession when he came to Jacob's home the day before. Henry inquired how much money, and Dan said approximately $1,600 to $1,700. Henry was not able to learn how Holcomb came to that knowledge.

The next witness was Officer George Mann of Jackson. He had arrived at the Crouch house about nine o'clock that morning and found a pocketbook upon the upper part of the bottom window sash in the room where Henry White and his wife lay dead. He opened the book and found $105 and a certificate of deposit for $500, payable to Jacob D. Crouch. He was told the pocketbook belonged to Eunice White and gave it with its contents to Coroner Casey.

Officer Mann reported to have found a bullet on the floor of Polley's room. When it was presented at the trial, he identified it. The bullet appeared to have struck the wall just above the bed and fell on the floor, where he picked it up.

Giles Hunt was the next witness. He lived four miles away and had arrived on the scene at nine o'clock. He testified that he had seen the tracks sworn to by other witnesses in the home and around the house and was certain they were made by a rubber boot or shoe. He also claimed he saw Judd Crouch with some shell casings in his hand, which he had said he picked up off of the floor.

The next witness sworn in was Harrison Snow. He testified that he arrived at the Crouch house at seven o'clock in the morning, and there were eight people there on the scene at that time. He first examined Mr. Crouch and found he was dead, then went into Polley's room and so on to all the other rooms.

He stated he looked for anything that was missing and claimed he could not detect anything that was. He was familiar with the family's way of doing business, as Crouch had paid him at different times. He reported that Eunice White had always taken charge of the papers. The mortgage he paid money on was in a long leather book, in which there were a number of other mortgage papers. He stated that during the time he was at the house, he witnessed Dan Holcomb take this book and the papers it contained and put them in his pocket.

Snow also claimed that the shot in Polley's breast was first discovered by a witness. He turned down the clothes before he found the wound, and it was his opinion that the shot had been fired when the bed clothing did not cover the breast but had been put over the body after Polley had been killed.

This leads one to believe that Polley was killed while getting dressed for bed. Perhaps while he was dressing, he heard the shots when Jacob opened the front door and was shot when he went to investigate.

Snow said that he helped search Mr. White's and Polley's clothing, and no money was recovered from the body or possessions.

George Boles testified next. His story of the trunk was disputed with the facts described earlier, but his testimony did not change. When challenged on this, the boy said he was terribly scared that morning and could not remember exact details.

The information about Dan Holcomb acquiring a .38-caliber pistol from the Marshall man was brought up in the trial. Holcomb claimed that he purchased the pistol for William Holcomb. In his testimony at the trial,

Henry Smith stated that he had later spoken to William Holcomb about the pistol being a present to him, and William did not know anything about it.

Fred Lonsberry and Charles Andrews, the boys who lived at the Holcomb residence, both testified to seeing Judd Crouch and James Foy with matching pistols. The only difference in the two black handles was that one was broken. They recounted seeing the two cleaning the guns at the kitchen table three Sundays before the murders, and the pistols were rusty. They also described hearing Judd and James shooting them later that day at a target.

## Hearsay and Witnesses

Throughout the trial, there was a tremendous amount of hearsay evidence admitted, which is something that would not be allowed in modern courtrooms. In one example, Henry Smith testified that he had heard Charles Wangelson, another associate of Holcomb, say that Dan stated he would not allow Eunice's baby to see the light of day. Dan was reported to have asked Charles if he thought Judd could do the murder. Charles had responded that it took a cool hand and a bull head to do such a thing and that Judd was too big a fool. Charles had claimed that Dan had replied, saying, "Judd is no fool by any means."

The prosecution brought up the close relationship of Judd Crouch and James Foy, along with Foy's behavior and death. Other evidence brought by the prosecution was the path through the wheat field between the Holcomb home and the Crouch home. In this path was supposedly discovered boot prints, which matched Judd Crouch's peculiar boot pattern.

On one day, the prosecution put on the stand "Uncle" Jacob Hutchins of Spring Arbor. He was brought in to testify that the boot prints were indeed those of Judd Crouch; however, when Hutchins took the stand, he either refused to answer the questions or feigned ignorance of the questions for hours.

When his answers did come, they were so irrelevant in nature to the questions asked, with such grimaces and flourishes, that the audience in the courtroom kept roaring with laughter, notwithstanding the admonitions from the court.

Eventually, the prosecution had one of Hutchins's nephews, who was more familiar with the man, question him. Although he initially resented the pleasantries in the questioning, Hutchins began to answer.

Hutchins testified he had discovered some tracks in the wheat field just after the murders and knew those boot tracks were made by Judd Crouch. He stated he had also shown these tracks to others, who agreed with him.

Hutchins also testified that Holcomb had sued him a few years before for $2,000 and that there was a woman at the bottom of the whole thing—it was all fabricated by Holcomb to bleed him of cash. He also stated that he did not care if the entire family were all sent to the penitentiary.

Other witnesses were brought to testify to the validity of the tracks as being made by Judd Crouch.

Another witness, William Hartupee, who owned a hardware store, testified that Foy was in his store four days before the murders looking to buy .38-caliber cartridges. Hartupee did not have any in stock, and when Foy walked out, he asked him, "Thirty-eight long will shoot stronger than short, won't they?" He told them they would. Foy replied, "That is the kind I want—that shoot the hardest."

A man named A.D. Pierce of Sherwood testified that he sold a .38-caliber revolver to a man who fit Foy's description in August or September before the murders. He recalled Foy saying he was "not going to stand any more talk from some at home, and wanted a revolver to fix them with."

Another man named V.A. Bennett corroborated Pierce's testimony, having been present at the exchange. He too believed the man fit Foy's description.

Hartupee was able to describe Foy in detail, but the court would not allow him to identify a photo of Foy from the undertakers in Jackson when the prosecution tried to present it.

A man named E.H. Howell also testified. He had spent the day with Foy before he made his trip to Union City. Foy mentioned to him that he had caught Detective Brown under the window of the Crouch homestead and told him that he thought there were two or three other people involved with the murder.

He stated that Foy told him that the "cat story" was a fabrication. This was an expression of the time referring to an old tale where a merchant sells a man a pig, but puts a cat in the bag instead and cheats someone out of their purchase. The expression "to let the cat out of the bag" also came from this fable.

From this claim by Foy, one is to presume the story by Henry Holcomb about the Canadian named Allen being involved was presented to investigators to be deliberately misleading. Foy also mentioned that if he did not have enough money, he knew where he could get some. From this,

Howell believed Foy had knowledge of the whereabouts of the money stolen the night of the murders.

Howell asked Foy what he knew about the murders, and all Foy would say was that he always went armed since the tragedy. He also said Foy had been drinking a lot and seemed nervous.

A man named Fred Knight of Union City was sworn in next. He testified that he had once seen Foy draw a revolver while a man named Colonel Sleed was standing with his back to him. Sleed had words with Foy the previous evening. Foy then hid the revolver when he noticed someone else saw him do this.

Samuel Burgett, a policeman, testified that he encountered Foy in Union City. Foy claimed to be there to sue Major Easton for slandering him in the newspaper. Foy had some words with Colonel Sleed, who was with him, and threatened to shoot anyone who bothered him anymore. He mentioned that he saw Foy at different times that day. He also reported that Foy had scared a witness to the shooting back into his house after he shot Elmer Shuler.

## Holcomb's Housekeepers

Ella Shannon testified in the Crouch murder trial. She was sixteen years old, and one week and a day after the tragedy, Judd Crouch and Dan Holcomb came to offer her employment as a housekeeper.

She stated that on the second day of her employment, she was preparing to do the family's washing following instructions by Mrs. Holcomb. She went upstairs, into the room where Judd and Foy slept, and discovered a pair of boots, pants and a shirt; the boots belonging to Judd Crouch were covered in a thick, slimy mud; the pants were also muddy and wet at the bottom and bloodstained at the top. There was blood soaked through the knees, and there was also a pair of drawers soaked in the same. She stated the shirt was splashed with blood on the breast and the sleeves. They were all bundled and hidden behind an old trunk, and after discovering this, she decided to put it back carefully where she found it.

She recounted how the bundle was taken away later that same day. She overheard Judd say to Foy, "By God Jim, we had better go upstairs and get our clothes and take them away." She claimed they went upstairs, each coming down later carrying a bundle, and left.

She also testified to a conversation she heard between Dan Holcomb and his wife, Susan, regarding the missing box of Crouch's papers. She stated she heard Mrs. Holcomb ask, "Where is that box of papers?" and Mr. Holcomb replied, "Never mind the box now; I have them all safe."

Apparently, Ella was so frightened with what she had overheard and witnessed that she left Holcomb's service and returned home to her parents. She kept her silence until the detectives got ahold of a clue that led them to her and they ferreted out her story.

The girl who worked there before Ella was Nettie Snyder. She had worked at the Holcombs' for ten days following the murders and was called by the defense to rebut Ella's statements. She testified she swept the room occupied by the two men, Judd Crouch and James Foy, two or three times after the murder and never found bloody clothing. She recalled finding one shirt for Judd and two for James, and both were entirely free of bloodstains. She also did not recall seeing any muddy boots.

Ella Shannon also testified that a detective hired by Holcomb came to see her and asked her to change her testimony. She refused. She then told the court the man told her that he advised her to go away or change her testimony, or she was liable to get shot.

She wept at the trial while relating this experience. When asked by the judge if she could identify or point out the man who said this, she pointed out Detective Baker, who was sitting at the defense table. She said that she refused to let him in her house. He had a gray horse and rode up in a buggy. He left after threatening her.

She also stated that after Byron Crouch arrived from Texas, the Holcomb family did their talking in a room behind closed doors. She heard them slide the door lock when they went in there.

Based on Ella Shannon's testimony, one can only wonder: Was Nettie Snyder telling the truth? Or was she threatened also? Or did Ella Shannon manufacture her entire story? The defense brought witnesses who attacked Ella's character, saying she was untrustworthy and her testimony should not be believed under oath. However, she was a sixteen-year-old girl. Would she really have been so bold as to lie to the courts? If she did lie, what did she have to gain from risking perjury?

## More Discoveries and Troubled Witnesses

Further investigation of the Holcomb house uncovered a large amount of Crouch's papers, including the box believed to contain his most valuable ones.

There were many other interesting developments as the trial went on and on, including Silas Sauders, a Black man who was on the long list of witnesses in the case against Dan Holcomb. He attempted to cut his own throat by making two large gashes on his neck. A patrolman in Jackson came upon him and prevented him from making matters worse. He was taken to a doctor, sewn up and sent home.

Another interesting witness, Charles Dekalb Harrington, testified that he first met James Foy about four years prior on board a Mississippi River steamboat. He was going downriver on a pleasure trip, and Foy was employed on the boat as a deckhand.

Harrington related how he witnessed James Foy kill a man while gambling on that steamboat. Foy escaped, and Harrington went on to California. He next saw Foy in Jackson four days before the murder; they met on the street.

The prosecution then wanted Harrington to relay the conversation he had with Foy, but the defense objected. The judge would not allow the testimony. Eventually, the defense allowed this later in the trial.

Harrington claimed that when he met Foy, he wanted him to enter a plot with him against Jacob Crouch. He declined and stated he had since been wandering about afraid for his life, using fictitious names.

Harrington was described as a Valjean (the principal character in Victor Hugo's *Les Misérables*) in the newspapers. Harrington had been accused of murder and many other crimes and once served two years in prison for assault with intent to kill. He had a history of blaming his own sins on the faults of others, according to the press.

Throughout the trial, and in the months leading up to it, there was a lot of animosity toward the press from both the Crouch and Holcomb families. Many of the family accused the press of spinning the news to reflect that it was a conspiracy by family members to kill Jacob Crouch and Eunice White. They claimed Crouch had made known his intentions of removing family members from his will. There were subtle accusations that Eunice had been manipulating him to do this, and Jacob planned to leave everything to her.

Rumors abounded that Jacob had made known he was cutting Judd Crouch, Susan and Daniel Holcomb out of his will, and since they all lived together, a plot began. Perhaps even Byron Crouch in Texas was involved, as he arrived shortly after receiving word of the incident, holding meetings in private with Judd, Susan and Daniel.

There were even letters written into the newspapers in Jackson confessing to the crime. This practice seemed to be typical of the day, perhaps a tactic applied by defense attorneys to sow the seeds of "reasonable doubt" and deflect a conviction of their clients.

Some letters were downright absurd, as in this example published on March 27, 1884, in the *Jackson Patriot*:

> *Dear Sir—I have a confession to make in connection with the horrible Crouch tragedy. Years ago, when I was young and living at home, I became acquainted with Jacob D. Crouch. I loved him, but he did not reciprocate. My love turned to hatred. I swore to have revenge. I swore to kill him, for nothing but blood would satisfy me. I have waited all these years for my revenge and I had it when I saw my victims writhing in the agony of death. Then I was content.*
>
> *I came to Jackson and bribed Foy to help me and with Foy's help I did the deed: and a part of my plan was for Foy to make a confession and to lay it onto someone so that it would make more trouble for the family, but my conscience troubled me day and night till I made this confession.*
>
> *After I left my victims it was not hard to cover my tracks in the fearful storm that was raging. I have been wandering from place to place, and now I am in the little town of Union City, and here I wrote and mailed this letter. It will do you no good to try and find me for before this letter reaches you I will be away. All the regret that I have is that I did not burn them and their accursed property. And now beware how you try to hunt me down, for if you do, you will die like the rest.*

Of course, no signature was contained in the letter.

The trial went on for several months. When concluded, the jury did not convict Daniel Holcomb. The case against Judd Crouch was dismissed following Holcomb's acquittal. As predicted by the county, the evidence in the case was entirely circumstantial, and any actual evidence had been contaminated by the crowds of onlookers and would-be sleuths who trampled the murder scene.

# UNSOLVED

Perhaps modern technology of ballistics, fingerprint evidence, DNA and a securing of the crime scene would have brought about a conviction in this case.

In the end, Jacob Crouch, Moses Polley, Henry and Eunice White and their unborn child were just the first deaths in this chain of events. James Foy and Susan Holcomb died of apparent suicide. Detective Galen Brown and Elmer Shuler were both shot but recovered. Silas Sauders attempted suicide rather than testify.

If this was not enough, one other bizarre incident happened during the trial. A local farmer named Lemuel Bean, the father of the county surveyor, living in Spring Arbor, attended the trial every day as it unfolded. One day, he had an emotional breakdown. He began racing his buggy up and down the street outside the courthouse. He shouted out loudly, one arm holding up a large rope halter that he had fashioned around his neck, screaming: "I am the murderer!" and the citizens should hang him. He knocked two policemen down as they tried to subdue him. Afterward, when questioned at the jailhouse, he recanted his claims.

The story occupied the news for two years.

Who killed Jacob Crouch and the others? Was it James Foy? Dan Holcomb or Judd Crouch? Did a group of thieves follow Moses Polley home? Did George Boles or Julia Reese have anything to do with it?

Or was it some other rogue group of criminals? Reports of robberies abounded during this time. The North Adams Post Office, just ten miles south of Jackson, had been broken into and the safe blown up a short time before. A store, a warehouse and two safes had been broken into in Jonesville, and another theft occurred in Hanover in the months prior.

However, the Crouch house was described as secure: "Among all of the residences along this road, this was the least likely to be selected by a stranger as the home of a wealthy man."

It is a fact that whomever did commit the crime certainly made off with a fortune.

It was also observed by the reporters of the time that no reward for the detection and capture of the perpetrators was ever offered by the family, who clearly had money. Many felt that this should have been done at the outset, but the relatives of Jacob Crouch remained indifferent to offering any reward.

The *Jackson Citizen Patriot* wrote:

> *Justice cannot overtake the murderers without man's help, and nothing should be left undone to secure that aid. Jacob Crouch toiled for years to amass a fortune; he gathered riches great in extent, and leaves a princely estate. Of this abundance a few thousand should be devoted to punish his foul and unnatural murderers. The old man should be avenged, and the blood of those slaughtered with him cries out for vengeance. The heirs of*

William and Eunice White grave site. *Author's collection.*

*this vast estate should devote part of it to aid the law. There should be no further delay in this matter. Thousands should be spent to punish the crime.*

The father of Henry White eventually put up a reward, along with Jackson County. The Pinkerton Detective Agency was brought in to aid in the investigation in the years that followed, but no one else was ever prosecuted for the crimes. Today, the murder remains unsolved.

## AFTERMATH

Byron Crouch returned to Texas and lived until 1920, passing away in San Antonio. He is buried at San Antonio National Cemetery.

Daniel Holcomb remarried, to Amanda Crouch, another member of the family. He moved to Wisconsin, passing away in 1920 at the age of eighty-eight. He is buried at Walnut Hill Cemetery in Baraboo, Wisconsin.

Judd Crouch moved into the Jacob Crouch home, remaining there the rest of his life. He married Viola Worrall, passing away at the age of eighty-six in 1946. He is buried at Woodland Cemetery in Jackson, Michigan.

Elmer Shuler recovered from his bullet wounds. He passed away at the age of forty in 1905. He is buried in Sherwood Cemetery, in Sherwood, Michigan.

Detective Brown also recovered, continuing in law enforcement. He is believed to be buried in Indiana.

Moses Polley, the visiting cattle drover, was buried at Reickert Cemetery in Transfer, Pennsylvania.

Jacob Crouch and Susan Crouch Holcomb were buried in Crouch Cemetery in Spring Arbor, Michigan. Jacob's headstone is no longer visible, or perhaps his grave was never marked.

The funeral for Henry and Eunice White drew over one thousand people; they blocked the streets, overflowing the porches and steps on either side of the church. Their coffins were carried in hearses led by a long line of carriages and wagons that took over a half hour to unload all of their occupants. They were laid to rest at St. John's Catholic Cemetery in Jackson, Michigan.

Today their monument bears this inscription:

*Wm H. White and Eunice his wife. Assassinated on the night of Nov 21, 1883.*
*How pure those hearts, how well prepared.*
*For the swift approaching shock.*
*Although unwarned, we know their hopes*
*Were founded on the rock.*
*Faith shows our treasures daughter, son,*
*Where hearts may trust their prize.*
*At rest in homes not made with hands*
*Eternal in the skies.*
*But the Good Shepard watches his own,*
*His power out sped the blow.*
*The stricken lambs lie on his breast*
*Our loved are safe we know.*

# 11

# THE LONESOME DEATH OF LIZZIE STRATTON (1884)

*The responsibility for the serious crime which led to the death of Lizzie Stratton seems never to be fixed with any certainty.*
—Kalamazoo Gazette, *March 28, 1884*

On Sunday, March 15, 1884, twenty-five-year-old John Stratton, along with his brother James, discovered the body of his sixteen-year-old wife, Lizzie, when he returned home to their wooden shanty in Alamo Township, near Williams' Station in Kalamazoo County. Lizzie Stratton lay with her back arched on a pallet of straw in one corner of the room, pale in the low light of the small dwelling. Her partially naked torso from her waist to her legs was streaked with crimson. Beneath her and around her feet was a large dark pool of blood.

Lizzie was the daughter of H.C. Rounds of Kalamazoo, Michigan. When the tragic news of his daughter's death reached Rounds, it was perhaps an even deeper blow than one might have expected. He had just lost another child to diphtheria the prior spring, and a few weeks prior his aged mother had burned to death in Hopkins Township when her home caught fire.

When Lizzie's body was found, neighbors heard of the gruesome spectacle and gathered around the shanty, outraged at the condition of the poor girl. The people were aroused to anger about the matter and demanded an investigation to find her killer or killers.

At the time the discovery of Lizzie's body was reported to authorities, Dr. Butler was sent for to conduct a medical examination. The prosecuting attorney of Alamo Township instructed Sheriff Gallegan to make a full investigation.

The autopsy revealed a sinister secret. Lizzie Stratton's death was caused by internal hemorrhage and shock as a result of an attempted abortion. Instruments for this were found at the scene. John and Lizzie had been married for two years and already had an eight-month-old child when it was revealed she was pregnant again.

# Investigation

The investigation was immediately launched to uncover whether someone had done this to her or whether she had attempted this on her own. Detectives were assigned to the case by prosecuting attorney Frank Knappen to assist Sheriff Gallegan.

John Stratton was born and raised in Alamo Township. His mother died when he was just one year old, and he and his three other siblings were raised by their father on a farm. His family was poor, and he had met and married Lizzie Rounds when she was just fourteen years old.

They lived in a shanty, which was a small wooden shed with plank board on the exterior, heated by a cast-iron stove, with very little insulation. The wooden floors were often uneven and the winters unbearable.

John Stratton denied any knowledge of how Lizzie came to her death. The investigation uncovered enough suspicion to persuade officers to charge him with her murder on April 2, 1884. Also charged was Lucy Stratton, his sister. They both languished in jail until the hearing, which was held a week later.

The trial lasted a week, with constant denials from John. He finally confessed to purchasing the instruments that were used in the attempted abortion that resulted in the death of Lizzie. The responsibility for who actually committed the acts that led to her death was never determined. John Stratton admitted only to procuring the instruments used. Lucy never admitted any knowledge of the incident. It remains a mystery today whether Lizzie attempted this herself or someone else was involved.

Was her tragic death a solo action driven by despair? Or was it a reckless collaboration with another to escape her troubles or, worse, a forced procedure to torture her? The investigative capabilities of the time yielded more questions than answers.

The charges against Lucy Stratton were dropped when John Stratton offered a confession to Justice Wattles in the Alamo Township courtroom during the trial. On April 18, 1884, John was sentenced to one year in the Michigan Reformatory in Ionia, Michigan. This was a state prison that had opened in 1877, initially used for high-risk offenders. It was regarded as extreme punishment to be sent to this facility.

Lizzie Stratton was buried in Hillside Cemetery in Plainwell, Michigan.

# 12

# THE BUTCHER OF DIBBLE HILL (1886)

*A hymn book laid under the head of Mrs. White, and her parasol was behind the stove, while her gloves were on her hands. On her breast laid a razor.*
—Battle Creek Daily Moon, *January 8, 1886*

On April 26, 1871, there was a joyous gathering hosted by Deacon Philip Reeve, a well-respected and successful farmer, and his wife, Jerusha, in Webster Township, Washtenaw County, Michigan. Friends and relatives were present to witness their daughter, Frances Ann Reeve, in her nuptial ceremony to Dr. Martin White.

Frances, twenty-five years old, was a schoolteacher. She had a fair complexion and a kind disposition and was well educated. Martin, twenty-six years old, had recently graduated from the Detroit Medical College on June 29, 1870. He was a short, thickset, bearded man with a nervous demeanor. When he received his diploma, he anticipated a brilliant medical career ahead of him. Together they left the old homestead Frances had grown up on with warm well wishes from family on their departure.

Frances had dreams as well. She dreamed of an affectionate husband, an ideal home and a long and happy life. The joy she must have felt when riding away from the family farm could never prepare her for the unfulfilled future that lay ahead.

Her wedded life was soon less than blissful and proved more sorrowful and troubled than she could have ever imagined. Martin became an overbearing, jealous husband in private, always upbraiding her whenever she spoke to another man in public.

Despite this, they had two children, Mary and Bessie. Both were beautiful girls and very intelligent. Their childish glow and sweet smiles were the only consolation Frances would know in her home, and this kept her going.

Dr. White moved his family around Michigan, trying to find success in his profession. At first, they settled in Davidson, in Genesee County. Later he opened an office in Ann Arbor and then moved to Dundee for a few years.

## ISOLATION

In July 1874, Dr. White made his journey westward, taking up residence in Battle Creek, Michigan. They had no family in the city, and Frances and the children endured the anger of Martin in isolation.

They first settled on Green Street. Later Dr. White purchased a lot on South Jefferson Street in an area then known as Dibble Hill and built a home. Dibble Hill received its name from its most prominent citizen in the neighborhood, Leonidas Dibble. Dibble, who lived across the road, was a highly regarded attorney who had established the Peninsular Railroad through Battle Creek. The Dibble home stood large on a slight hill. The

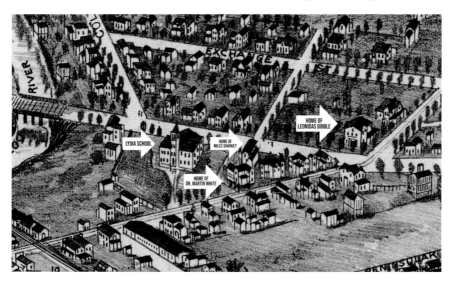

Bird's-eye view 1880 map of Dibble Hill. *U.S. National Archives*.

house Dr. Martin White built was only partially completed when the family moved into it and took several years to complete.

As soon as their Jefferson Street house was finished, the doctor built another larger home on the rear of that lot facing Lydia Street. He moved into the new home and rented the smaller one to Miles Sharkey, a clerk at the Grand Trunk Railroad. In November 1886, Martin made arrangements with the Sharkeys to switch homes, as the Sharkeys were in need of more room. The Whites needed more rent money. Martin's medical practice was struggling. Swapping homes was a mutual advantage.

In 1876, Frances's father, Philip Reeve, passed away. Her mother, Jerusha, came to visit them, per the 1880 census. It is likely that she brought the estate settlement information to her daughter.

Russell Reeve, Frances's brother, later explained that financial matters of the Reeve family were kept away from Martin. Russell considered Martin was "partially deranged, and was not capable of handling money with any degree of safety." The property in Washtenaw County was kept in Frances's name for this reason and any other financial matters kept private.

Her mother and brother and other family members had offered Frances and the children shelter against the abuse of Martin, but she always declined, endeavoring to remain a true wife and keep the family together.

The doctor was not considered by those who knew him to have strong skills for making acquaintances. His medical practice did poorly, and the only patients he did see came to him from the lower economic class—mainly because they could afford no one else.

Martin was described as conceited and one who had great faith in his own ability as a doctor, yet somehow he was not considered a skillful physician. Despite this, outwardly he was never regarded as a vicious man. He was not characterized to be overly intelligent and was sometimes observed to be irritable in temper. The littlest matters seemed to vex him.

Outwardly, his jealousy of his wife was noted by many, as was his occasional cross demeanor toward her. He limited her access in the community to her weekly visits to the grocer and Sunday's attendance at the Presbyterian Church. Their two girls attended school at the Lydia Public School, which was next door to their home. Outside of brief walks to school, the children were seldom seen by their neighbors. Frances took pride in her yard and garden and was frequently seen tending it.

Despite Frances's limited interaction within the community, it became known that Martin was always trying to find out how much property she owned. Frances had received money from her father over the years, which was how they managed to survive, as Martin brought home very little.

Once, her father sent her $1,000 in bonds, another time $1,200. Both times Martin made her sign them over to him and liquidated them. Neighbors learned of the incidents by overhearing arguments coming from their house. Money seemed to always pass through Martin's fingers, and he was in a constant state of anxiety about this.

When her father passed away, Frances received word from family of her inheritance, which included large parcels of real estate. Martin locked her in a room in their home, refusing to let her out. He denied her food and water until she capitulated in signing the deeds over.

Frances, however, was clever enough to sign over only the smaller parcels to him. When her brother, Russell, heard of this, he confronted Martin and demanded he deed the property back over to his sister. Martin refused.

Notwithstanding all of this treatment, Frances endured. Without complaining to others in the community, she submitted to the demands of her husband. She made few acquaintances, and she seldom called on her neighbors. Neighbors, likewise, seldom called on the White home.

Martin then began making frequent trips to Washtenaw County by railroad, following his father-in-law's death. During the week between Christmas and New Years 1885, he traveled to Ann Arbor to liquidate the final pieces of property she had deeded to him.

Longtime lawyer and judiciary Judge Benjamin Franklin Graves served in the Michigan Supreme Court from 1868 to 1883 and had recently returned to private life living in Battle Creek in 1884. In mid-December 1885, Martin visited the home of Judge Graves, who later said about the visit: "I was not acquainted with him, but he appeared to know me. He said he had resided there for years, and he was a practicing physician, and gave me his name."

Martin asked Judge Graves for business advice. He told him that his wife's father had died, leaving a farm near Ann Arbor, which his wife had an interest in. He told him he had sold one piece of the property, but there was another piece that he had sold that had wheat planted on it. Another party owned the shares of this. He had not disclosed this to the buyer when he had sold it and feared he had done a great wrong.

He also expressed other title concerns regarding other parts of the property that dated back to 1840 that had tax liens on it, but he had sold the land anyway to another party and guaranteed the deed. He expressed fear that the purchaser would come back on him with a claim for damages.

Judge Graves noted, "He seemed greatly troubled about it. I was struck by his peculiar actions and conversation. I had difficulty in making him understand. He appeared confused and laboring under depression of spirits. He handed me a dollar upon leaving, saying 'perhaps that will help some.' I had the impression at the time that the man was foolish or insane, and so remarked to my wife."

Although the details of the land transactions made by Martin White are not precisely known, it is clear that Philip Reeve owned 240 acres of land in Dexter, Michigan, in 1864. Only 100 acres of that land, including the house, was owned by his son Russell Reeve in the 1896 parcel maps. The 140 acres of the remaining farm were deeded to other family members and sold following his death; 20 acres were sold to T.R. Stanton and 120 acres went to Linval Ward.

Martin had returned from Dexter with $300 and deposited this money in the City Bank just before Christmas.

On Sunday, January 3, 1886, at around one thirty in the afternoon, Martin White stopped by the home he rented to Miles Sharkey. He spoke with Mr. Sharkey concerning the payment of some rent money, mentioning in the conversation that the funds went to support his family. He then asked permission of Miles to go upstairs to get a medicine chest he had stored. One room upstairs had been reserved by White in the lease for use as storage for various articles. Miles and his wife later described Martin as acting nervous, but also noted his behavior was often peculiar. He came downstairs a short time later with the trunk, leaving the house.

The Whites' house was built very close to the home the Sharkeys rented, and the kitchen windows of each faced the other. On Thursday, January 7, Aaron Hall the grocer knocked on the door of the Sharkey home and asked Mrs. Sharkey if she had seen any of the Whites. He told her Frances had taken some baskets from his store to carry groceries home and not returned them. He had gone over to the house and knocked on all the doors for a few days now, but no one seemed to be home.

# A GRUESOME DISCOVERY

The next day, Friday, January 8, Mrs. Sharkey became suspicious that all was not right in her landlord's home. The curtains had been drawn all week, and no smoke appeared to be coming from the chimney. It was a very cold January, with temperatures well below freezing. She instructed Miles to go over to see Mr. White and discuss the rent with him. Miles went over and knocked on the door, rang the bell and, after a time, returned home, informing her they were not home.

Curious, she decided to investigate for herself. She went through the back gate of the home and peered in a rear window. Looking between gaps in the curtain, she thought she could see spots of blood on the floor, as well as blood on a child's apron that was lying there. She returned to her home and prompted her husband to go over there and make further investigation.

Miles Sharkey reluctantly went over to the Whites' house in the company of his neighbor Frank Courter, a local artist. They discovered the doors all locked from within, with curtains drawn all around the house. On one side of the house there was a woodshed, which had a window. They were able to open this and crawl through, gaining access to the kitchen door. When the two men peered through the partially opened kitchen door, a horrible sight met their gaze.

On the floor in front of the cookstove lay the bodies of Martin and Frances White in a pool of blood, with their throats cut. They both lay frozen and dead. The men stood for a moment in shock and horror.

Frank then exclaimed, "Where are the children?" and ran up the stairs, leaving Miles standing in the kitchen. He bounded down moments later crying aloud, "Oh my God! They are murdered!"

Miles followed him back up the stairs, and there on the bed lay little Bessie, aged five, with her throat cut. Mary, aged twelve, lay on the floor in a large pool of blood with a similar gaping wound to her throat.

The two men quickly left the home and raised the alarm with neighbors. Miles spoke to a man riding past in a wagon to notify the first officer of the law he came upon of the discovery.

Sheriff John Barber, who was also the proprietor of a livery stable near the Michigan Central Depot not far away, arrived on the scene soon after. The coroner Alexander Briggs was called, who then assembled a coroner's jury of six prominent businessmen, and the investigation began. The news of the tragedy spread rapidly throughout the city, and soon the sidewalks were lined with people on their way to see for themselves. Horror draws a crowd.

# Investigation

The scene in the kitchen was the first studied in detail. Mrs. White was wearing a black cassimere dress and had on her outdoor wraps, rubber boots and gloves. Partially underneath Mrs. White lay a hymn book, *Songs of Christian Praise*, open with the cover facing up. Her hair was disheveled and matted in blood, blood besmeared over her face, head and clothes. Later, when her body was moved, a set of false upper teeth fell from her clothes.

A short-handled axe covered in blood lay behind a cookstove, next to a parasol. On the top of the stove was a bread knife with blood on it. Blood was all over the floor and on the wood pile beside the stove. Someone appeared to have used the wood to scrape blood off something.

There was also a chair, a table and a highchair marked with splatters of blood. The handle to a cupboard had smears of blood on it as well. There was a pail on the floor of the kitchen filled with frozen bloody water, as if someone had washed their hands. Beside the pail was a blood-soaked mop with stains on the handle. Lying beside the wash bench, next to the basin, were two bloody one-ounce vials on their side. One was full and corked and the other nearly empty.

Looking from the kitchen to the sitting room just through the door on the right-hand side of the floor lay Mrs. White's black straw hat. A trail of blood led from the nearby bedroom to the kitchen, where Martin and Frances were found. There were also drops of blood found leading up the stairs and large blood spots on the carpet in the front chamber.

Drs. Simeon French, Arthur Kimball and Austin Alvord were called in to thoroughly examine the bodies of the deceased. It was determined that the younger daughter, Bessie, had been hit with a blow from the butt end of an axe and had her throat cut. The older daughter, Mary, had two marks, one on the top of her head and the other on the back. Her throat was so badly cut, her head was nearly separated from her body.

Frances's head bore the marks of a severe blow to the back of her skull from the butt of the axe and a deep gash on her chin and cheek made from the blade of the axe. Her throat had also been cut with a razor, and a broken piece of the razor was found in her hair near the back of her neck. The back of her middle finger on her left hand was gashed through her glove and skin, about one inch deep. An open shaving razor lay across her breast.

Martin's head bore no marks of having been struck by the axe. His throat had apparently been cut with the small sharp blade of a three-inch pocketknife, which was found underneath him. His body was found lying partially on top of Frances.

# Discovery and Findings

Dr. Alvord testified at the inquiry that Mrs. White and the oldest daughter both struggled with the killer. He had known Frances White since 1858, meeting her first when he was attending studies at the University of Ann Arbor. He had described her as being a quiet woman with a yielding disposition. However, she fought back aggressively during this attack. Drs. French and Kimball corroborated Dr. Alvord's assessment.

The last person seen from the White family was Martin, when he visited the Sharkeys and picked up the trunk. The coroner's inquest determined that the deed had been committed forenoon of Sunday, January 3, the day Martin had last been seen.

The time of day was determined by what they observed in the house. The beds for the children had not been turned down. The older daughter, Mary, still had paper in her hair, which during the Victorian era was a hair curling method where women twisted their hair around paper to form ringlets when dried. The papers would be removed in the morning.

The theory was the beds had been made after they got up in the morning. The girls appeared to have been in the process of getting prepared to go to Sunday school. They had not been seen at Sunday school, which they attended every week at noon. Bessie wore a worsted plaid dress with a pink checkered apron. Mary, the older daughter, wore a black worsted dress and black stockings and had not gotten to the step of removing the paper from her hair before going out.

Frances appeared to have just returned from morning church service and reportedly had not been seen at the evening service. She was known to always attend both services weekly.

The coroner concluded that Martin White had murdered his two children upstairs in their bedroom, killing Mary first and then Bessie. He probably struck Mary, who fell down but was still moving and perhaps got up to fight back, so he hit her a second time. He then struck Bessie, who lay motionless after she was hit.

He then waited in surprise for Frances in the kitchen and struck her from behind. She likely fought Martin, who then delivered the blow to her face. Sometime after this, Martin sought out a razor, which he remembered he stored in his medical chest. He washed up and then visited the Sharkeys, arriving around one thirty in the afternoon.

When he returned to his house with the medical chest, he took out the razor and cut the throats of his two daughters to make sure they were dead.

Headstone of Frances Reeve. *Author's collection.*

Mary apparently was not, as the coroner saw evidence she had thrashed around on the floor when he examined the bloodstains.

After finishing upstairs, he returned to the kitchen and applied more force to make sure Frances was dead with his cut, breaking the razor. It was speculated that he tried to cut his own throat with the razor's broken blade, could not and then tossed it onto his wife's body.

He then picked up the bread knife from the kitchen and went into the bedroom. While standing in front of the mirror, he attempted to cut his own throat. However, the blade was dull, and he could not get a deep cut. Blood drops were found in front of the mirror.

He returned to the kitchen, tossing the bread knife onto the stove. Following this, he reached into his pocket, remembering he had a pocketknife. They found blood smears from his hand going inside his pocket. This time he was successful in cutting his own jugular and collapsed on the floor of the kitchen.

# Rumors and Theories

Despite these conclusions based on the investigation, there were still many other contrary facts discovered when they interviewed neighbors, compared with the evidence.

Did Martin actually kill his daughters first before visiting the Sharkeys and then returned to wait for Frances?

Had he really committed all three murders before visiting the Sharkeys? Was the reason for getting the trunk to get the razor, or was it to pack it away as part of his plan to escape?

Another fact that throws the conclusion into confusion is that an ex-marshal, William Hogue, testified that he had encountered Martin White coming out of a hotel in downtown on Wednesday night. He had stopped and talked to him for a short time. Hogue was specific about the date and time, as it was the only time he had been in town that week. He had attended a meeting with a service club. Did Martin kill his family and then stay in the house for three days before finally killing himself?

Sheriff Barber took possession of a trunk at the crime scene. It was packed as if for departure. It contained the medicine chest, which he had gotten at the Sharkeys', along with medical books and other articles.

Is it possible that Martin committed the crime and was planning on departing the country before fear of detection or remorse drove him to suicide? Perhaps his encounter with Hogue had sparked this fear in him of being found out.

Miles Sharkey told the coroner that Martin White had told him back in September that he was going away and rents should be paid to his wife. He stated he had his own living to make and left town for some time, then returned. Apparently, he had a falling out with Frances, and she told him to leave. It was later learned he had been in Jackson.

Following the murders, speculation circulated in the city that Martin White was a cousin of Henry White, who had been killed in the Crouch tragedy just three years earlier. There were even rumors that Judd Crouch had been seen in town visiting with Martin White, wearing a disguise so as to go undetected. Charles Barnes, the editor of the *Sunday Morning Call*, stated that the family connection with Henry White was not based in fact. He had contacted the father of Henry White and confirmed there was no relation.

However, Detective O'Neil from Jackson told the *Detroit News* after the incident happened in Battle Creek that he knew Martin White. He said the doctor had come to see him about a year ago with a lot of theories on the

Crouch murders. Martin seemed to be disgusted because O'Neil would not accept them. This story was likely the source of the rumors.

There were those who speculated that Martin White could not have killed himself, as the cut on his neck was made ear to ear, which would have been very difficult to do. Their theory was that someone killed him in front of the mirror and then dragged his body over to lay it where it was found in the kitchen.

Reverend George Chipperfield from the Presbyterian Church was confident that Frances had been in attendance at the evening service on Sunday, although other members did not see her. The absence of light at the house reported by neighbors on that Sunday led some to believe that Martin was killed first and the assailant waited for her to return home, then murdered her in the dark. However, it was more likely that the reverend confused which service Frances had attended when he considered it a week later.

When Sheriff Barber testified at the inquiry, he concluded from the investigations with the doctors that Martin White had killed his family. He first murdered his two daughters while his wife was at church, went to the Sharkeys' and returned to murder Frances. He then killed himself.

Within the trunk, Barber found that it was packed with Martin White's papers, articles and wearing material. Among the papers were deeds to property made over to Martin from Frances bearing that they would revert back to her or her heirs after his death. Martin had sold some property on his recent trip to Dexter and received $300 in payment. The trunk contained a receipt for $280 from the City Bank, indicating it had been deposited in Frances's name. Another $20 bill was found crumpled up inside Martin's clothing, along with a few other smaller bills. Other rumors that circulated after the tragedy was that Martin White was from Canada and had plans to return there before deciding to kill himself. The truth is, no one in the community really knew where Martin White originally was from, as he never said.

Other facts surfaced following the tragedy. It was revealed that Martin White was addicted to opium and morphine. On the day before the murders, he was reportedly seen in a drugstore that evening gossiping with the clerk, in a nervous state. In parting, he told the clerk he needed to go home and look after his babies. No bloodstains were reported as being seen on him at the time.

Of the two vials that Dr. Alvord found at the scene, the full one contained strychnine, and the mostly empty one contained lilac oil. It could be that White took the bottle of lilac oil, thinking it was the poison. When it did not kill him, he commenced to cutting his own throat. Perhaps he was in an agitated state withdrawing from the opium.

An addiction to opium would explain a lot of his erratic behavior that witnesses, neighbors and even the Reeve family had described.

His continuous financial problems and failing marriage, compounded by his declining medical practice, likely the result of the drug abuse, could account for a lot of his bewildered emotional state.

# Aftermath

Russell Reeve, the brother of Mrs. White, arrived on the train from Dexter on Friday evening, the day the bodies had been discovered. He was accompanied by his family physician, Dr. W.E. Ziegenfuss, who along with the three appointed doctors to the inquiry examined the bodies. Coroner Briggs released the bodies of Frances, Mary and Bessie over to Russell, but he wanted nothing to do with the body of Martin White. He left him to the undertakers to bury in the Potters Field with what little money they found in the house. Frances, Mary and Bessie were buried in the cemetery behind the Webster Church in Washtenaw County.

Webster United Church of Christ in Washtenaw County. *Author's collection.*

After the word of murder-suicide spread across Michigan, Martin White's brother, John White, from Flint learned of the news. He sent a telegram to the sheriff's office, with instructions to hold Martin White's body until a family member could arrive. He sent his son, who was also named Martin White, to Battle Creek on the first train available.

When the nephew arrived, he explained that his uncle Martin White and father, John White, were natives of County Clare, Ireland. Martin had arrived in the country when he was ten years old with his older brother and father, who were his only family members. Martin had a falling out with his brother when he renounced Catholicism, as John was very religious. Following this, Martin left when he was seventeen and attended medical school.

Later, when Martin White was practicing medicine in Davidson, Michigan, their mother died. John paid thirty dollars for her tombstone, and Martin, at that point a doctor, had agreed to pay for half of it. However, he never did. This caused a further estrangement between the two brothers. After Martin left Davidson, they had not spoken.

During the Victorian era, it was customary to travel in one's best clothes, especially when attending to matters such as funeral arrangements for a family member. Originally, when the nephew of Martin White arrived in Battle Creek, he was dressed in coarse farmer's clothes, stating he had been sent right from the farm by his father.

At first, it was believed he was instructed to bring the body of his uncle back to Flint, Michigan. Instead, he hired legal counsel to represent their family in the interests of the property of his uncle. Apparently, John did not care about what happened to Martin's body and determined he did not deserve a tombstone like his mother. The nephew eventually left town, leaving the body of Martin White with the undertakers.

One newspaper wrote on January 17, 1886:

> *As no one claimed the body of* [Martin] *White, it was buried in the Potter's field in Oak Hill Cemetery. The majority of our citizens desired that it be sent to the pickling vat at Ann Arbor, and have an examination made of the brain. The sum of $27 was found in his pocket book, and this was sufficient to pay the burial expenses. It was claimed the body could not be sent to Ann Arbor.*

The house where the family was murdered was kept under lock and key by the sheriff department in the weeks that followed. The neighbors who lived in proximity were afraid that someone would torch the house one night and imperil their properties. It had been a true house of horror, and other than the bodies being removed, the blood remained.

The home, because of the stigma of the horrible event, was considered valueless. The elementary school adjacent had expressed interest in the land. The neighbors appeared by mid-January to be rallying financial support to have it destroyed and the land given to the school.

One columnist of the time wrote: "Let's have it moved to a secluded spot and burned."

In the modern day, the site where the home once stood is now a parking lot. There are no longer any homes, and only commercial buildings and asphalt stand where the horror took place.

Few today have even heard of Dibble Hill, much less the story of the butcher who committed the unthinkable

## 13

# THE ADOPTION AND MURDER OF NELLIE GRIFFIN (1891)

*Nellie was a bright handsome girl, but as she grew in years, she also grew in waywardness....She would be found at all hours of the night hiding in dark stairways and some other out-of-the-way places, and was a continual source of torment to the neighbors.*
—Jackson Citizen Patriot, *February 12, 1891*

The Michigan State Public School for Dependent Children was believed to be the only one of its kind in the world when it was first officially opened in 1874. It was a combined school and asylum established and maintained by the state that per its charter "admitted all dependent children who have no efficient supporters." In the 1870s, the word *asylum* was the common term for an orphanage, which, in its literal sense, meant "place of safety."

## ORIGIN

Asylums (or orphanages) for children had existed before this point in history in the United States, and some indeed included education, but most were supported by private charities. Michigan was the first to establish a combined state-funded school and asylum. The chain of events that led to its establishment began with newly elected Governor Henry Baldwin in 1868, who appointed a commission to study and research legislation that might bring relief to county poorhouses relative to dependent children in the state.

The report gave the number of children under sixteen years of age in the poorhouses, providing a vivid picture of the lamentable conditions in these facilities. It was revealed that children in these institutions were kept in close contact with the adult inmates of both sexes, who were "the physical, mental and moral wrecks of their own excesses."

When the legislature convened in 1871, the important matters of this special commission were brought to light. It was revealed that under the existing system of poorhouses within the state, dependent children became criminals when entering adulthood, because in these institutions the innocent and criminal were treated alike. The outcome of these sessions resulted in the first draft of improvements in the penal and reformatory institutions of the state and a new proposal for aid for dependent children.

On February 22, 1871, a new bill was passed by both the Senate and the House and signed into law by Governor Baldwin on April 17, 1871. An appropriation of $30,000 for a new state school was included, and commissioners were appointed to locate it, erect buildings and take charge of the institution.

A beautiful site in the pleasant surroundings of Coldwater, Michigan, was selected one mile north of the city. Further appropriations were made in 1873, and the school officially opened on May 21, 1874.

Almost immediately following the opening, children were rapidly sent from counties in all parts of the state. Children were admitted between three and fourteen years of age, on the certification of the judge of probate of the county from which they came. They would remain in the school until age sixteen, provided homes could not be found for them before that time with private families.

The school consisted of a large main administrative building in the shape of a cross, three stories high, that included classrooms, dining rooms and employee and superintendent accommodations. It also included several cottages two stories high, forty feet by thirty feet, which could house thirty children each in dormitories, along with room for a manager. In less than a year, the accommodations of all the buildings were exhausted.

About one-third of the children were too small to work, but every child large enough was put to work two to three hours per day either on the farm, in the laundry, shoe shop, sewing room or knitting room or performing some domestic work. Each child then attended school for four

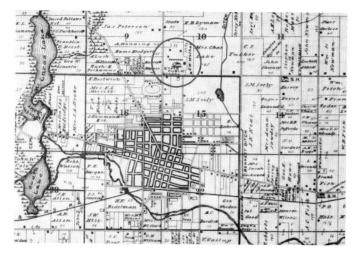

*Left:* State Public School in 1894 Atlas. *U.S. National Archives.*

*Below:* Baby Cottage, Cottage Row, State Public School, Coldwater, Michigan, circa 1890. *Courtesy of the Branch District Library.*

Baby Cottage, Cottage Row, State Public School. Coldwater, Mich.

to five hours per day, six days a week, with chapel on Sunday in various religious denominations.

The object of the school was to provide temporary support until they could be placed in families willing to take them. The governor appointed some thirty agents across the various counties of the state to find homes for these children and to see that they were well treated when placed within them.

# ORPHAN

Nellie Griffin was one of the many children whose circumstances in life led her to being placed in the Michigan State Public School for Dependent Children in Coldwater. She was born in September 1881. Her mother, Della Griffin, was a twenty-one-year-old servant working at the Clark house in Mason, Michigan.

She had become acquainted with Oliver Griffin, who worked in a carriage factory. He was described as a simple-minded son of wealthy parents, and she married him.

The marriage was filled with trouble, especially after Nellie was born. Oliver had an accident at the carriage factory, and his hand was cut off. He could no longer work, and they fell on destitute circumstances.

After a few years, Della could bear it no more. She left one day looking for work and never returned. She moved to Grand Rapids, leaving three-year-old Nellie with her father. Oliver too departed from Nellie's life, leaving her behind to live with his parents, as he headed west to California. He never returned.

Nellie's grandfather was the first mayor of Mason after it had been incorporated as a city. He also owned a farm and a considerable amount of real estate within the city. He was regarded by those who knew him to be a somewhat rugged, although wealthy man in Eaton County.

Nellie was a bright girl, but as she grew in years, she also grew in waywardness. Neither her father nor her grandparents seemed to have any control of her. Nor did they exercise any discipline. At all hours of the night, she would slip out of the house and wander the neighborhood. She hid out in dark stairways and out-of-the-way places, becoming a continual torment for the neighbors.

It was these same neighbors who became roused at her behavior, and after getting nowhere with her grandparents to discipline her, they solicited the authorities in Mason to intervene. They succeeded in having Nellie turned over to the superintendents of the poor in Eaton County after inducing Mr. Griffin, her grandfather, to sign a complaint after considerable pressure. Nellie was sent to the state school when she was eight years old, arriving there in 1889.

# THE RUSE

In January 1891, a man arrived at the Coldwater State School claiming he was from Jackson County. He met with Superintendent Newkirk, stating his name was George Hendershot, representing himself as a thrifty farmer and a Christian man. He claimed that he wanted to adopt a young girl and offer her a good home.

Newkirk called the county agent in Jackson, inquiring about Hendershot, and asked the agent to investigate him. He left instructions that if he could give any reason why he should not let the child go with Hendershot, he should telegraph him before noon on Wednesday. It was understood in that conversation that if he did not reply or contact Newkirk, that the superintendent would consider Hendershot acceptable and release the child to his care.

No telegram arrived before the train arrived at noon on Wednesday, and Nellie was allowed to depart with the man. She had officially been adopted.

The man's real name was not Hendershot. It was Russell C. Canfield, and he was neither a farm owner nor any kind of property owner in Jackson County. In reality, he worked as a laborer on a farm in Eaton County for a man named Harrison near Dimondale, Michigan.

He had originally lived in Lenawee County, where he was married for twenty-seven years. His wife had left him for another man. She said to him as she left that she wished she had departed twenty-seven years before. He divorced her, remarrying an older woman, who soon after left him as well. However, he never divorced his second wife.

After his second matrimonial failure, the chagrined Canfield sold his business interests in Lenawee County and moved to Charlotte, Michigan. Shortly thereafter, he began working for the Harrisons on their farm. When neighbors learned of his past and also observed his fondness for young girls, he was the source of many jokes, which he appeared to take good-naturedly.

In the Victorian era, marriage in many ways was a status symbol. A man's ability to secure a wife was considered a sign of maturity and manhood. Creating a family was often a sign of accomplishment, during a time when people were scarce. For a man's marriage to end in divorce was a mark of failure socially but could be overcome. A man who failed at two marriages was a social pattern unheard of, and it reflected poorly on him as a husband.

Deep inside, Canfield was humiliated. His sensitivity to the jokes of his neighbors compelled him to make a last desperate attempt to secure a wife. After a time, he came up with the plan to adopt a girl. Then after she had grown to sufficient age, he would marry her. With this, he thought it would put an end to the annoyance of neighborhood gossip concerning his unsuccessful endeavors to secure a wife.

After his ruse in convincing Superintendent Newkirk of his authenticity as Hendershot, he departed Coldwater with ten-year-old Nellie Griffin. Together they rode the railroad to Jonesville and then changed trains heading north to Dimondale.

## MURDER

Somewhere after they departed the train in Dimondale, walking up the road in the direction of Harrison's farm, is when Canfield realized the foolishness of his plan. He could never take her to Harrison's as his adopted daughter, nor could he marry her, as he was still married to his second wife.

With this realization, he departed the road, taking Nellie into the woods to the banks of a river. He then revealed his plan to her. She immediately went into great distress and wept bitterly. She began begging Canfield to take her back to Coldwater. Ignoring her pleadings, he struck her down in desperation and choked her to death. Or so he claimed.

Nellie's body was found later the same day by some men walking near the river. It was January, and Nellie's nude body was floating on the ice. The coroner was called, and a photo was taken of the girl, then circulated around Dimondale. A conductor on the railroad happened to see the photo and recognized her as having traveled with a man who had gotten off at the station earlier that day.

The description and the direction he was walking led them to the Harrison farm. Canfield was taken into custody and brought to the county jail. At this time in history, crowds gathering around a jailhouse were known to take justice into their own hands, via a lynching, whenever a heinous crime of this nature was committed.

## CONFESSION

Canfield knew he was caught. He also knew if he was released from the jail, he would be delivered to the mob. He confessed his guilt, writing out a statement, saying he had only choked the girl. He claimed he took her clothes off and then tossed her into the river, but he never violated her. He stated he buried her clothes under the floor of a cow stable at the farm. The clothes were indeed found there wrapped in a bundle.

The investigators, with the help of the railroad, had retraced the travel pattern of Canfield and discovered the girl had been taken from the Coldwater State School. Superintendent Newkirk was notified of the girl's death, and he arrived from Coldwater and positively identified Canfield as being the man who claimed to be Hendershot. He took Nellie's body back to Coldwater for burial.

Canfield was placed under armed guard by Sheriff Paddock to prevent the crowd from breaking into the jail. He had been arrested on a Tuesday, given his confession and taken to the magistrate the same day. He was sentenced to life in the Jackson prison and sent there in less than eighteen hours.

The swift justice was more likely the result of the growing crowd outside the jail. News had gotten out that Canfield's claims to have never abused or violated Nellie Griffin had been disproven when the medical examination was completed on her body.

## Outrage

Superintendent Newkirk became the target of community and statewide outrage for having carelessly allowed the child to be released into the hands of a man using a fake identity. After much public pressure, he tendered his resignation to the state legislature.

An official inquiry was held by the board of control of the State Public School, and after they conducted their investigation, they refused to accept his resignation. They stated, against the outrage of an inflamed public across the state, that Newkirk was not at fault, as he could not have foreseen that Canfield was "cunning and crafty" and deceiving him.

The board cited Newkirk's prior unblemished reputation of tireless work to the institution, and he was retained as superintendent.

The *Detroit Press* was outraged at this decision, repeating over and over in columns in the months following that Newkirk and the Board of Control of the State Public School were accessories to the rape and murder of Nellie Griffin, stating that her blood was on their hands. The newspaper upbraided the superintendent: "Newkirk's violation of the law led to the slaughter of a ward of the state."

They further chastised the board for upholding Newkirk's actions as giving a wink to the act and demanded the entire board be abolished, maintaining that they were the real murderers of Nellie Griffin.

In April of that year, under the direction of Governor Edwin Winans, the Board of Control of the State Public School was consolidated with two other state boards. The commissioners serving on the original public school board were released.

Della Griffin learned of the death of her daughter after reading about it in the newspaper. She had not seen Nellie in seven years, and it was the first time she learned she had been at the Coldwater State School.

Canfield was interviewed in prison by a *Detroit News* reporter in late February 1891. It was his first visitor in a month since being placed in solitary confinement in cell number 110. He rambled on from inside his cell about his family history, trying to drag out the interview to avoid being alone, and periodically pleaded to the reporter to ask the warden to assign him to a work detail. Upon leaving, Canfield was last seen pressing his face up against the cold iron bars of his cell, begging the reporter to tell the warden to take him out of solitary, his voice echoing down the east wing of the prison.

The reporter would later write: "There he stood as if to watch for the coming of the days which should take him out of the solitude and the company of the phantom face of his victim, the girl whom he killed and threw into the river."

# 14

# THE GHOST OF
# FARRAND'S BRIDGE (1893)

*The last Tunison saw of Johnson, his head was bowed and the horse was going along with no guiding hand. Then the wagon and horse became a mist, darkness settled over the earth, and the slowly moving vehicle was swallowed up by the great pine trees which line the roadway.*
*—V.C. Severance, 1895*

The village of Colon, Michigan, was established in 1832 by two brothers named Schellhous who dammed the Swan River and built a sawmill. Today, this village is known as the "Magic Capital of the World" for the legacy of magicians who came from the community.

Just to the north and west of Colon, there once stood an old-fashioned farmhouse. It did not differ materially from others in the area. There was a wide front porch, a well from which water was drawn and the usual outhouse buildings and sheds.

The house was surrounded on every side by fields of wheat, and the cattle they had was the best that could be found. Within the house, rag carpets covered the floors, a few cheap printed pictures adorned the walls and seating consisted of many old split-bottom chairs. On the center table in the "best room" could be found a copy of *Pilgrim's Progress* by John Bunyan, along with a family photo album, a few songbooks and a Bible.

Such was the home of the Swartz family. For years, this house was noted for its hospitality, and many a weary traveler rested within its doors. Those who called at the house noted the beautiful face of a charming young girl, the only daughter in the household, Dottie Swartz. She had two brothers, Dall and Forrest Swartz.

Dottie's brother Dall was considered a wild sort of fellow. His reputation in the rural neighborhood was not the best growing up, often regarded as the local pest. When an act of meanness was discovered in the area, either an act of vandalism or a mistreated animal, roads always seemed to trace back to Dall.

On one occasion, Dall left home for more than a year, tramping around the country, stealing rides on freight trains and begging for food from door to door. He finally landed in Kansas, where he remained for some time.

While he was away, Dottie became acquainted with a man named Willard Johnson from Burr Oak. Johnson came from a well-known family and was respected. Dottie's parents were pleased with their relationship, encouraging her to marry the promising young man.

During the time they were courting, Dall had become homesick and made his way back to Michigan. Discovering his sister was courting Johnson, he became quarrelsome with her and seemed to take a dislike to him. There were several outbreaks between the two men during this time.

By March 1888, it was thought that all ill feelings between Dall Swartz and Willard Johnson had been wiped out. Willard and Dottie were married, and Johnson leased his father-in-law's farm.

However, the conflict between Dall and Willard was far from over. Soon after settling on the farm, the men had a violent quarrel that finally terminated with Dall driving Willard from the yard with a butcher knife. This was just the beginning of the hostilities between Johnson and the Swartz family.

Shortly after the trouble, Willard purchased a farm in Burr Oak, south of Colon, and took up residence there. Dottie was away from home, visiting her family a greater part of the time, but Willard made no complaint about this. During this time, they had a daughter, whom they named Bessie.

Within a few years of moving to Burr Oak, Dottie became ill. Willard took her to Mississippi for the benefit of her health. Several letters were exchanged between the family in Michigan and the Johnsons while there, but it was later learned that Dottie's mother could not read, so all of the letters were being read to her by Dall.

Although the letters were mere updates on Dottie's progress, Dall convinced his mother the letters demanded she go down to Mississippi, and so she did. A short time later, she returned with Dottie. Willard remained behind in Mississippi to settle some business.

In the meantime, back home, Dall attended a medical college. When Willard Johnson returned from Mississippi, Dall informed the couple he had appointed himself as his sister's physician. This was not really satisfactory to Willard, but he remained quiet rather than cause another disturbance with the Swartz family.

While "treating" his sister, Dall induced her to move into his home and leave her husband. When Dottie did so, Dall always made any visit by Willard to see his wife contentious. The tension between the two increased day by day.

The last serious trouble occurred on September 18, 1893. Dall, who professed to be a physician, claimed that Johnson owed him a bill for taking care of his wife. He brought suit, and judgment was given to him by the courts in the amount he demanded.

On October 12, Willard left his home early in the morning, starting on the twenty-two-mile drive in his buggy to the home of the Swartz family. The object of his visit was to make a settlement with Dall over the matter of the court judgment and see his wife and child.

On his way, he stopped by the home of Forrest Swartz, the youngest son in the family, and told him of his plan. Forrest told him that it would be useless to go, as there was no way Dall was going to settle with him.

Undaunted, he made his journey anyway. When he arrived, he learned that Forrest was right. Dall was obstinate. They were unable to come to terms of a settlement. Neither would he permit him to see his wife and child. With a heavy and frustrated heart, Willard made his long drive home, alone.

Along the way, he stopped at the home of a neighbor named Cy Tunison, telling him of his experience and troubles with his family relations. Tears were in his eyes as he told the story. Tunison attempted to console him, but without success. Slowly, Willard buttoned up his coat and, with a look at the low, threatening clouds in the west, directed his team and wagon back onto the road.

A detective who later investigated the case wrote about his departure: "The last Tunison saw of Johnson his head was bowed and the horse was going along with no guiding hand. Then the wagon and horse became a mist, darkness settled over the earth, and the slowly moving vehicle was swallowed up by the great pine trees which line the roadway."

# Farrand's Bridge

Farrand's Bridge was built in 1868 and named in honor of the family that had at one time lived nearby and given the township access to the land. It spanned the St. Joseph River at a picturesque spot, and it was built at a time when there was no railroad into Colon. It was a fixed arch–type bridge, with steel rods that supported the roadbed. It was the main passage in this area, one and a half miles north of Colon, over the river. In the present day, this bridge was torn down and rebuilt in 1965 with a more modern structure.

On the night Willard Johnson left the home of his in-laws in his return to Burr Oak, Mrs. Kemmerling, whose farm was adjacent to the river, was out chasing after her cows near the bridge. For some reason, the cows had failed to come back home that evening, and at dark the tinkle of the bells could not be heard.

She started out looking for them, and it was very late by the time she had found them—much later than people in the area typically were out. It was half past eight o'clock when she drove the cows back across the bridge, getting them back into the stable. Fifteen minutes later, when she was milking the cows, she heard four shots ring out in the darkness.

The next morning, on Friday, October 13, 1893, a body was found floating in the St. Joseph River just below Farrand's Bridge half hidden beneath the weeds. The body was that of a man, drifting in about four feet of water, and he was in a sitting position. Nearby on the bridge, a revolver was found with four chambers empty. It would be hours before anyone was able to identify

Farrand's Bridge, circa 1895. *St. Joseph County Historical Society.*

the man. After the coroner arrived with Sheriff James Manbeck, the body was pulled from the river and laid on the bridge.

Upon examination, it was discovered when the shirt was removed that he had been shot four times on the left side of his body near the heart. This had to have occurred prior to him being thrown in the river, based on where the gun was found. Soon after, a neighbor who gathered at the scene identified the man as Willard Johnson.

## Rumors and Suspicions

A hush fell over the crowd that gathered at the bridge that morning when the body was identified. Then, an old man stepped up from the crowd, saying aloud:

> *Friends and neighbors, many of us have known Johnson for years, and not one of us ever heard of him doing an evil deed. He was everybody's friend, and would rather cut off his right hand than harm a human being. His dead body lies before you. He has been murdered; killed by a cowardly assassin. For what purpose, I do not know, and do not care. He is dead, and the voices of his neighbors cry out for vengeance. We must find his murderer, and when we do, will deal with him as he has dealt with poor Willard.*

Members of the crowd then cried out: "You are right! We will lynch him!"

The words from the old man had a magical effect on the people present. They all scattered and returned carrying all kinds of weapons, from old-fashioned horse pistols to the latest revolvers. Crowds were sent east, north, south and west. In a short time, they were scouring the woods and fields in search of the murderer.

The sheriff appointed Deputy Ralph G. Dock in charge of the investigation. He had been a member of the American Detective Agency and had done training on how to conduct an investigation.

His first conclusion was that one could rule out a suicide, as he deemed it impossible that Johnson could have shot himself four times in the side and then jumped off, as the gun had been found on the bridge.

He also measured wagon tracks approaching the bridge. The object of the crime apparently was not robbery, but murder, as $27.36 was found inside his pockets along with a silver watch, a lot of money for that time. Also,

Johnson was not known to be a quarrelsome man, so his having gotten into a fight with someone at that hour was not likely. Deputy Dock was forced to admit that the murder case was a perplexing one.

Mrs. Kemmerling had relayed hearing the shots but also told the deputy about hearing a wagon drive away shortly after. She was able to identify the color of the horse as being gray and believed she saw two men in the wagon. She also remembered seeing a peddler with a white horse on that bridge a few days before and wondered if he may have been the culprit. Despite this information, the deputy was still left with a mystery when he finally departed the crime scene later that day.

## Swartz Suspected

Following the autopsy, the body of Willard Johnson was removed to his mother's house. It was a short time later that Dall Swartz, accompanied by members of his family, arrived at the Johnson home, appearing terribly shocked and asking if they could do anything. At one point, Dall offered to sit up with his body during the night. Willard's mother declined, knowing full well there had long been hostility between the two men. She did not consider Dall's offer to be sincere, nor did she believe her son would want to have him watching over his body.

Although Dall appeared to shed bitter tears of grief over Willard's death, many members of the Johnson family remembered that Dall had once threatened to kill him—including the time he chased him with a butcher knife.

Willard's sister went so far as to accuse Dall in front of the entire family; she thought his killer was under the same roof that evening. Dall was quick to admit he had an argument with Willard earlier in the day but that he also had witnesses who could prove his whereabouts the night of the murder.

Regardless, suspicion soon pointed to Dall Swartz as Deputy Dock investigated. Johnson was known to be separated from his wife, Dottie, and she was living in the home of Dall Swartz. There had been a recent lawsuit between the two, and the considerable ill feelings that had developed between both parties was common knowledge. Additionally, Johnson was returning from a confrontational visit at the Swartz home the night he was murdered.

Deputy Dock learned that when Willard arrived at the Swartz home that day, Dall was in the field and was called in by the dinner bell. When he arrived, he became confrontational with Willard, asking him to surrender his revolver before any negotiations would be considered. Willard did so. Even though he had all but offered to settle the entire amount of the judgment in installment payments, Dall refused to concede and agree to any terms. Deputy Dock also learned from interviewing Dall himself that there was no indication that Willard was ever given his firearm back when he left for home that evening.

Initially, the deputy assembled a case against Swartz, as the family was known to have a gray horse. Within a few weeks of the investigation, Dall Swartz was brought up on the charge of murder, along with another man named Mel Rockwell, a worker on the Swartz farm and a presumed accomplice. Deputy Dock arrived at the Swartz farm and arrested the two men, driving them to the Centerville jail in a wagon. The entire way, he nervously expected the two men to try to jump him, but instead they professed their innocence the entire journey.

Prosecuting attorney Robert Akey believed the case was too big for Deputy Dock to work on his own, so he hired two detectives from a private agency to assist him. The investigation lasted several months and even included having one of the detectives get a job at the farm of Forrest Swartz to find out information about his brother.

Detective Stumpfler posed as a man who was secretly fleeing a murder he had committed in Indiana. After the detective in disguise told the story to another farmhand, the father of Dall Swartz, the sheriff's department arranged to come arrest Stumpfler and take him to the jail.

They placed Stumpfler in the cell in Centerville right next to Dall Swartz and Mel Rockwell. The other detective, V.C. Severance, was to be arrested on a bogus charge of forgery and secured in the same jail. The intent was to see if one or the other could build trust with Swartz and Rockwell and get a confession. What they unraveled was a spider's web of intrigue.

Detective Severance made the most progress in getting information, first from Rockwell and then Swartz. Swartz, in an effort to prove his innocence, offered a $100 reward for information leading to the arrest of whomever had killed his brother-in-law. Swartz at one point became so convinced of Severance's authenticity as a friend that he signed a contract indicating he would pay him the $100 he had set as reward money if he could help him pin the crime on someone else.

When Dall Swartz willingly confided in Severance, he unknowingly exposed his own mother to being part of the cover-up of the crime. She would later admit that Dall had left the home that evening for a few hours, and she did not know where he had gone. Dall's mother even allowed Severance

V.C. Severance, circa 1895. *Annis Burk 1895.*

to copy all of the letters of correspondence between their attorneys and the Swartz family, which he presented to the prosecution.

In the meantime, Deputy Dock had discovered the true location of the crime scene as not being on the bridge itself, but farther down the road, based on additional testimony of other neighbors who also heard the gunshots that night. In finally locating the site of the murder, he could see a scuffle in the dirt in the road and wagon tracks cutting across an open field that a local farmer confirmed were not made by his family.

Prior to the trial, Severance visited Dall, Mel and Dall's mother in the jail in Centerville, revealing to them he was a detective. Dall's response was to collapse in grief inside his cell, burying his head in his pillow. Mel's response was similar. His mother's was vengeful. She threatened to scratch his eyes out.

## SWARTZ ON TRIAL

The trial was held in Centerville, Michigan, in May 1894. Dall Swartz was put on trial first. Throughout the proceedings, Swartz maintained his innocence.

Although the dispute between Swartz and Johnson was known, there was no physical evidence linking either Swartz or Rockwell to the crime. Thus the entire case was built on circumstantial evidence, compiled by the investigation of Deputy Dock and the two detectives.

During the trial, the detectives, Severance and Stumpfler, observed that the Swartz family always ate at the same counter in the diner across from the courthouse every day at lunch. They spoke with the owner of the diner and asked permission to hide inside the counter. He agreed.

On one lunch break of the trial, they hid for two hours while the Swartz family ate lunch and talked next to them. Although cramped, they noted down a lot of valuable information, which they turned over to the prosecuting attorney.

There were a few pieces of testimony in addition to what has already been covered in this story that greatly helped the prosecution.

One was a farmer who had followed two men in a carriage the evening of the murder coming from the direction of Colon, driven by a gray horse. When the carriage finally pulled off the road, it had done so at the Swartz farm. It was then that the farmer recognized Dall Swartz as being the driver. He also noted the horse was hot and steaming in the cold night air, which was evidence it had been driven hard.

The other testimony came from a witness who swore that Dottie Johnson, the widow of the murdered man and sister of Dall Swartz, had deeded all her property over to Dall before the death of her husband. This being clearly defined for the jury, the only obstacle between Dall getting all of the property was Willard Johnson.

Another story that surfaced during the investigation was a witness's description of a man seen that evening on the bridge riding a white horse. The man was reported to have paused on the bridge, looked out at the river

Detectives securing evidence at the diner illustration from "The Johnson Murder." *Annis Burk 1895.*

and then moved on. The identity of the man was not uncovered by Deputy Dock or the detectives and lingered as a mystery.

After a lengthy trial, the jury deliberated for a period of about six hours and returned with a verdict of guilty of murder in the first degree. Dall Swartz was sentenced to the Michigan State Prison for life by Judge E.L. Yaple. Rockwell was tried following Swartz a few months later, but he was acquitted.

## Sheriff Seekell

Even though Swartz was serving a life sentence in Jackson Prison for the murder of Willard Johnson, the sheriff of St. Joseph County was asked by the Swartz family to look into the case.

Sheriff James Wesley Seekell reviewed the investigation that led to the conviction of Dall Swartz. In reviewing the case, he held the idea that the prosecution had rushed to trial in the murder of Willard Johnson and that an innocent man may have been punished for the crime.

One of the mysteries about the trial was the mention of the man on the white horse who had been seen on the bridge that night. He had also been described as being seen in the area in the days preceding the murder. Who was he?

With time, Sheriff Seekell believed he was able to trace down the identity of the man with the white horse seen on the bridge. His name was Henry A. Cowen, and he had been discovered to have been someone the sheriff at White Pigeon had been looking for on swindling charges.

Apparently, Cowen had been representing himself as an advance man for a circus, taking people's money and then leaving town. Sheriff Seekell became suspicious that this criminal may have been the one who committed the crime, as he traveled on a white horse.

The sheriff was finally able to track down Henry A. Cowen in Cambridge, Illinois, in 1895, with the help of private investigators paid for by the Swartz family. He brought him back to Centerville for questioning.

The white horse rider had been a conspicuous mystery surrounding the trial, and the sheriff was convinced he had his man. He even reported to the newspapers in Three Rivers at the time that he intended to charge Cowen with the murder of Willard Johnson.

However, after a lengthy interrogation, Cowen was able to prove his whereabouts that night with a clear alibi. He was nowhere near the region where the murder had taken place. While in custody, from all of the stress

The murder of Willard Johnson illustration from "The Johnson Murder." *Annis Burk 1895.*

of the interrogation, Cowen had a massive heart attack and was transferred to a hospital.

Sheriff Seekell, despite the setback of Cowen as a suspect, remained suspicious that the real murderer was still out there.

## A TRAMP CONFESSES

A year later, a tramp in South Haven, Michigan, made a confession to another tramp around a campfire in early August 1896. He confessed to having murdered Willard Johnson and watching another man go on trial for the crime he had committed. He was tormented by the thoughts, as he maintained he was a Catholic, and could not bear the thought of someone else being punished for what he had done.

At first, the other tramp thought this was another tall tale around the campfire and did not give it much consideration. However, a few days later, he wandered into the sheriff's office at South Haven and relayed the story he had been told.

The tramp who had told the story was John Crowley. He was located and brought to the sheriff's office in South Haven by deputies. After a short interview, without pressure, he openly confessed to the murder of Willard

Johnson. After Crowley put his confession in writing, Sheriff Seekell was sent for, and he came to take him into custody, escorting him back to Centerville.

John Crowley confessed that he had first met Willard Johnson earlier in the year in July, when he had called on his house and requested lodging. Johnson had refused him a room, ordered him off his place very forcefully, beat him up and threw him off the property. Crowley had left that encounter bitter and angry at the mistreatment. He claimed he swore to Johnson before leaving that he would get his revenge on him.

It happened later that year in October that he was walking along the road outside of Colon when he saw Willard Johnson traveling in the opposite direction in his buggy. He hid beside the road, waiting. When Johnson arrived at his location, Crowley stepped out and shot him. He did not know how many times he had fired but knew that he had hit him multiple times.

When Johnson collapsed, Crowley climbed aboard, pushed the lifeless man aside and drove the buggy to the bridge. He then rolled him off the bridge into the river. He had hoped the body would get caught in the current and float away; however, it got caught in the weeds not far from the bridge. He then fled the county and made his way to South Haven, fearing someone had heard the shots or had seen him.

The written confession was taken to the judge, and Crowley, after being charged with murder, waived his right to a trial. He was convicted of the murder of Willard Johnson and sent to the Michigan State Prison. A few months later, Dall Swartz was pardoned by Michigan governor Hazen S. Pingree when a formal request was filed following the Crowley conviction.

# REVIEW

Some news reporters of the time implied that the Swartz family paid Crowley to make the confession, to free Dall. However, Sheriff Seekell maintained that the earlier conviction of Swartz was a rush to judgment and the Crowley confession was sincere. He found the details of his statements aligned with the facts of the case, believing Crowley truly had made a conscientious decision to not allow another man to be punished for his crime.

In 1902, Dall Swartz took the sheriff's office to court to recover his one-hundred-dollar reward. After his conviction for the crime, his money had been transferred to the sheriff's office. Despite having spent two years in prison for a crime he had not committed, he only wanted his reward money returned.

The mystery of who really murdered Willard Johnson is a confusing tale of intrigue that may never be fully unraveled. All circumstantial evidence pointed to Dall Swartz at trial, with witnesses seeing him returning home with the same gray horse that other witnesses had described.

Who did Mrs. Kemmerling see on the bridge that evening? Both scenarios allude to motive.

Crowley's description of his encounter with Johnson did not seem to align with the character of the man as described by those who knew him. However, in the weeks before his death, Willard Johnson was enduring a lot of stress effectuated by Dall Swartz. Could it be he mistreated a wandering Crowley?

Lastly, who was the man on the white horse?

Dottie remained living at the home of her parents. Her daughter, Bessie, grew up as a bright and happy child. When she became older, one can only wonder if she was ever told the truth of how her father had died and that her own uncle was once convicted for the crime.

An 1895 story written about Farrand's Bridge alludes to the location being considered haunted since the night of the murder, claiming none dare venture there after dark anymore. Wild, despairing cries are said to rise from the dark, sluggish waters that flow beneath the bridge.

Could it be the spirit of a man sitting in the weeds, longing for his wife and daughter?

## 15

# COINS FOR A HORSE

## THE MURDER OF
## LEROY ROGERS (1894)

*Tefft came after the horse, acting as if in a hurry to get away,*
*and he paid for the horse in a lot of small change.*
—Marshall Daily Chronicle, *May 26, 1894*

Leroy Rogers was a farmer who owned forty acres just west of
Hastings, Michigan, in Rutledge Township. He lived alone and
worked hard on his farm but was not a prosperous man by any
means. He had endured a difficult life but in 1894 at sixty-two he was still
a durable spirit in good health.

Leroy served in the American Civil War with Company D, Sixth Michigan
Infantry, enlisting at the beginning of August 1864 and was discharged
later the same month. After the war, he was married and had a son, Levant
Rogers, in 1867. His wife passed away, and in 1880 he moved in with his
brother in Allegan, where he made money as a laborer on local farms while
raising his son.

After saving his money, he purchased a forty-acre farm in Rutledge
Township, Barry County, just west of Hastings, Michigan. His brother
Edwin purchased his own farm in the township not far from Leroy around
the same time. His son had grown and moved away by then, starting a family
of his own. Leroy lived the solitary life of a farmer, as an old bachelor.

On Sunday morning, January 7, 1894, Edwin, who resided nearby,
stopped by to see Leroy. He had heard from a neighbor that his brother had
a visitor two hours before. When he walked into Leroy's house, a scene of

carnage was the last thing he expected to find. Leroy was lying on the floor near the stove against a backdrop of horrific slaughter.

An axe was buried deep in his neck, pinning him to the floor. His head had been crushed just above his eye with what appeared to have been the butt of the same axe. Later it would be discovered when his body was being prepared for burial and his clothes removed that he had three bullet holes in his stomach.

The shocking discovery was framed in an eerie silence, amid the popping sounds of a fire within the kitchen stove. His body was still warm. The murder would have had to have occurred just a few hours before. The room showed evidence of a terrible struggle, with furniture tossed about and sprays of blood across the walls, windows and floor. Edwin ran to the neighbors to raise the alarm, returning only to lock up the house. A neighbor sent for the coroner. Leroy's son, Levant, was sent for in Kalamazoo.

The coroner, Dr. Woodmansee, arrived an hour later. After examining the scene, he organized an official inquiry panel to investigate the crime. Edwin and Levant, who had arrived a few hours later, informed the coroner that Leroy was known to collect old coins, and the coins were missing. Levant reported that he had given his father a tobacco sack two years prior, which he kept all of his coins in, and the sack was nowhere to be found. Missing also from the home was a .38-caliber pistol. The same size rounds were later found inside the victim.

The immediate conclusion was that Leroy Rogers had been murdered, with the motive being robbery. His family and neighbors were dismayed, as Leroy had not been a wealthy man.

During the investigation, it was revealed that Leroy Rogers was a very private man and would not allow a visitor into his house unless he knew them. Thus, their initial list of suspects included immediate family. The investigators interviewed Edwin extensively and also Levant, and both were cleared of suspicion.

# THE COUSIN

A few days before the murder, on Wednesday, their twenty-four-year-old cousin Asa Tefft from the town of Martin, in Allegan County, stopped by Edwin Rogers's farm and stayed for a few days at his home. Asa informed Edwin he was visiting a girl who lived nearby. Asa also told him that later in the week he was going to Hastings to handle some business. Edwin informed

Asa that he was going to drive his team to Hastings on Sunday and he could ride along with him in the wagon. Asa declined the invitation, instead leaving on foot for Hastings on Saturday afternoon.

When the investigators learned of the cousin's visit, they went in search of Asa Tefft. Their suspicions heightened when they found a pair of rubber boots that were determined to have belonged to Asa covered in blood in some bushes near the township of Irving just a few minutes north of the crime scene. The investigators learned from interviewing residents in the area that Asa had been seen on the road between Hastings and the farm on that fateful Sunday. They also learned that he made a hasty departure from Hastings.

They finally caught up with Asa at his home in Martin. When they searched his residence, they discovered the .38-caliber revolver and sack of old coins, which had blood splatters on it. When they examined Asa's clothing, they found fifteen spots they believed to be blood. Asa Tefft was arrested and charged with murder on the following Monday. The trial officially began in May 1894.

At the trial, Asa and his family hired a defense attorney. The prosecution had a lot of witness testimony and material evidence that all pointed to Asa being the murderer, but it was largely circumstantial. After being charged with the crime, Asa had remained silent the entire time he sat in jail. He refused to speak with investigators, as his attorney had advised him not to. Thus, he remained hushed throughout the trial.

## THE TRIAL

At the trial, a neighbor, Mrs. Charles Francisco, swore that on Saturday night before the murder, she saw someone pass her house. She also saw the same man the next morning walking rapidly going east away from Leroy Rogers's house. She testified that his size and appearance resembled that of the defendant, Asa Tefft.

Another neighbor walking on the same road that night, John Brown, testified to passing a man meeting Asa Tefft's description going in the direction of Leroy Rogers's farm on Saturday evening.

Two other men testified, Robert Ironside and his son Fraser, to walking past Tefft on the road coming into Hastings in the early hours of the morning on Sunday. They said the man darted past them rapidly with his face turned away, as if he was afraid to be seen. They described his clothing, which was close to what Tefft was found wearing when he was arrested. However, it was just before dawn with low light conditions, and they could not positively identify him.

Further evidence was revealed that Asa Tefft's purpose for going to Hastings was to pay for the keeping of a horse that he owned, as he owed boarding fees at the livery stable.

Bert Phillips, the livery owner, was placed on the stand and testified that Asa Tefft had shown up on Saturday night and tried to get his horse away from the stable without paying. Phillips caught him in the act and chased him off. Phillips then locked up the horse in the stable, to prevent Tefft from trying it again.

The next morning, Phillips said Asa showed up with a bag of several odd coins and paid for the horse. The investigators discovered that the payment made to the stable was done using old coins, similar to the collection known to be at the home of Leroy Rogers. He said Asa seemed to be in a hurry to get away and impatiently waited as the stable owner counted out the payment. Phillips then released the horse and Asa left.

Dr. Lowry, along with Professor Vaughn from the University of Michigan laboratory in Ann Arbor, testified that they had found blood on Tefft's clothes. When they asked Asa Tefft if he had washed his clothes, he first denied it, and then admitted sponging them down with ammonia and water before he returned home to Martin.

Dr. Lowry found 160 stains on the pants, and they were all tested for blood. A majority of them came back positive as being human blood. Tefft's defense attorney later argued that the stains came from Asa when he had a nosebleed.

Before an attorney had been found for Asa Tefft, a wealthy man from Galesburg, Samuel Carson, came by the jail and had an interview with him. He offered to help Asa out with financing a defense if he could tell him where he was the night before and on the morning of the murder. Asa had responded, "You can't help me out; blood has been found on my clothes." Mr. Carson withdrew his offer of financial help. He was permitted to testify on behalf of the prosecution, detailing his encounter with Asa.

Levant Rogers was brought in to testify. He confirmed that the bag found in Asa Tefft's possession was indeed the one he had given to his father two years earlier and Leroy had kept his coin collection in it. He explained that his father was a collector of odd-looking coins, not just old ones.

Edwin Rogers was also put on the stand for the prosecution, and he confirmed that the bag used for coins that was found in Asa Tefft's possession was indeed the one his brother owned. Edwin was grilled in cross-examination by the defense attorney on what he found the morning he discovered the body of his brother. He described in detail the location of the blood spots, the location and condition of the articles in the room, the doors, the cupboards and windows when he arrived. Despite the pressure, Edwin maintained a steady tone in all of his answers and never contradicted himself.

During the trial, the defense filed a motion to have the jury dismissed. It was learned that the bailiff and sheriff had been approached by members of the jury and asked to see the defendant in jail to ask questions of him. This was an unprecedented request. Thinking they were being helpful to the jury, they complied and brought them all to the jail.

When they arrived, the jury foreman asked Asa Tefft, "Have you made peace with your God? Would you not like the prayers of Christian people?"

To which Asa responded, "Yes, if they have a mind to make them."

When Asa told his defense council what had happened, the attorney then filed the motion to dismiss the jury. The judge was prepared to declare a mistrial and start the process all over again, when members of the Tefft family approached the defense attorney to confer. They told the

Leroy Rogers's headstone. *Author's collection.*

attorney they could not afford to pay for a second trial and asked him to not object. With this, the defense begrudgingly withdrew the motion to have the jury dismissed.

On May 31, 1894, the jury, after deliberating for six and a half hours, returned with a verdict of murder in the second degree. The judge sentenced Asa Tefft to thirty years in prison. Tefft took the verdict coolly, never losing his nerve, which had sustained him through the trial. He was taken to the State Prison in Jackson the following day.

Throughout the trial, Asa made no attempt to explain where he was the night before or the morning of the murder. He remained silent during the entire trial, only occasionally speaking in whispers with his attorney.

The murder was determined to have been motivated by robbery and that Asa had attacked Leroy with an axe. Then, when Leroy was on the floor, Asa found the pistol and shot him three times. Asa then tossed the house, leaving with the bag of coins and the gun, returning to Hastings at a desperate pace to pay for his horse.

After reacquiring his horse, he returned to Martin, disposing of the rubber boots along the way. He may have believed he was in the clear when he reached home, not realizing he had left a trail of evidence like breadcrumbs to his own door.

Asa Tefft died in prison in 1920 at the age of forty-two. He is buried in Hicks Cemetery in Watson Township, Allegan County, Michigan.

Leroy Rogers is buried under a Civil War headstone marker in Rutland Cemetery, in Hastings, Michigan.

# 16

# IN COLD BLOOD

## THE MURDER OF JAMES ROBINSON (1894)

*James Robinson, an aged man living alone about eleven miles southeast of the city,*
*disappeared Saturday evening.*
—Hillsdale Standard, *July 17, 1894*

On February 11, 1894, thirty-four-year-old Alton Misenar married Daisy Belle Smith in Coldwater, Michigan. Daisy was just sixteen years old. They moved into a home in the southeast corner of the city. On July 7, 1894, Daisy who had just recently turned seventeen, went to spend Saturday night at her father's farm, leaving Alton alone at home. When she returned on Sunday morning, she had to rouse Alton by rapping on the door and calling his name, as he was sleeping. The front door was locked, which she found unusual. They never locked the door. They lived in a rural area and seldom had any visitors. At first, Alton refused to let her in, telling her to go away and return later. This she found very odd and persisted knocking, demanding he open the door.

After much persuasion on her part, he eventually came to the door and unlatched the lock, letting her in. Once inside the house, she ventured into one of the bedrooms and saw the lifeless body of an older man lying on the floor. She did not recognize the man. Alton steered her away from the room, placing his hands on her shoulders, and told her not to say a word about it. He told her that the man was a tramp who had attacked him and he had killed him in self-defense. Daisy was shocked at this revelation. Speechless, she went into another room to process what she had just heard.

He then carried the body down to the cellar, where it lay until Sunday night. About an hour after sunset, he carried the body back up the stairs, disappearing through the front door into the night, carrying a lantern. Daisy was not sure what to make of all of this, but she wanted to believe her husband and so followed his orders to remain silent. She did not follow him to see where he was going. Nor did she broach the subject again with him. She was relieved the body was no longer inside her home, but she was vexed by the experience, which continued to haunt her.

Alton went out to the north side of the barn that was near their house. He lay the corpse down, went into the barn to grab a shovel and proceeded to dig a trench eighteen inches deep. He then rolled the body in. He tossed the little dirt there was from the hole on the remains. Instead of relying on just dirt to conceal the burial, he covered the body with fresh manure taken from inside the stalls in the barn and a nearby pile in a field. He hoped this would mask the smell of decomposition, deterring anyone from looking underneath it.

# The Missing Neighbor

During the week that followed, a seventy-five-year-old man named James Robinson, who lived alone on a twenty-five-acre farm in Section 34 just south of Coldwater, became noticeably absent. Robinson, although somewhat of a loner, was always a familiar sight working around his property and in the fields. Days had passed, and no one had seen him.

By Friday, the concerns had mounted, and two neighbors went to his home to see if he was in trouble or perhaps had fallen ill. They knocked on his door, and no one answered. They went inside his house. He was not in any of the rooms. This is when the mystery began, as searching further around his farm, he was nowhere to be found. For three days, people in the community searched the roads and fields around his farm and the nearby countryside to see if they could locate him. Robinson remained missing.

On Sunday, the week following Daisy's encounter with her husband inside the home, Alton Misenar showed up at the Robinson farm when neighbors were organizing another search. He presented a bill of sale to a group of men standing on the porch. He told them Robinson was gone and claimed the papers he presented to them were signed by James Robinson. The documents deeded the entire property, including harnesses, horses, crops and so on, over to him. He told them that Robinson had approached him to sell his farm and stated that he was moving to live with his son in the northern part of Michigan quite suddenly, and Alton had purchased the land.

The neighbors were in disbelief. They could not believe Robinson would sell his farm without mentioning it to anyone else, much less leave the community without saying farewell to those who knew him. It was out of character for the man they had known for years. On Monday morning, the men reported the matter to Sheriff Hezekiah Sweet in Coldwater, requesting he investigate.

Hearing the rumors while in town about the missing farmer, Daisy Misenar showed up at the sheriff's office the same day. She told her story to the sheriff of what she witnessed her husband doing the week prior.

With the combined information from the neighbors and the testimony from Daisy Misenar, the sheriff and his deputies began to search the Robinson farm and the land around Misenar's home. They eventually discovered the manure pile near the barn and unearthed the body of James Robinson.

Feeling like she had betrayed her husband, Daisy became overcome with despair and grief. She was a newlywed less than six months, and her husband was most definitely going to be convicted of murder.

On July 12, overwhelmed by the events and the sudden collapse of her marriage, Daisy Misenar attempted suicide by taking strychnine. Fortunately for her, people in proximity came upon her after she had ingested the poison and gave her prompt medical attention. She survived, later telling others she was sorry that she did it.

The autopsy on James Robinson's body revealed he had been struck on the head by two different instruments: a blacksmith's hammer and also an axe. They searched the home of Alton Misenar and discovered the murder weapons, which had been wiped off but still showed traces of blood on them. They also discovered bloodstains on the kitchen floor inside Robinson's home that had been partially washed off. Alton Misenar was taken into custody and charged with murder.

# THE TRIAL

The trial of Alton Misenar did not begin until February 1895. Ironically, it began on the eleventh, the one-year anniversary of his wedding.

The bill of sale was determined to be a forgery, and this was brought up at trial. The murder weapons were presented as evidence, as was the discovery of blood on the kitchen floor and Robinson's body in proximity to Misenar's home. The trial lasted sixteen days. Daisy was compelled to testify, as were several of the surrounding neighbors.

Misenar did not have a strong defense, although he attempted to portray that he was insane during the trial. He freely admitted he killed James Robinson and shouted frequently during the trial, to bolster his insanity defense. He was described as making grotesque gestures in his personal habits, as an attempt to appear animalistic in behavior.

The prosecution made a strong case that he was not insane but a cold, calculated murderer. They made sure it was clearly known that this was not self-defense, as Misenar had claimed. It was presented through the testimony of neighbors that he had known Mr. Robinson and been friendly toward him in the past. Misenar's entire motive appeared to be simply to steal the property of the man.

On the final day of the trial, the courthouse was packed with a tremendous crowd, all wanting to be on hand to witness the outcome. After a forty-minute deliberation, the jury returned with a verdict of guilty of murder in the first degree. Misenar's face was reported to have turned pale white when the jury read the verdict, and he nearly collapsed in exhaustion.

When he was returned to his cell, the sheriff made a search of the space before securing him for the evening. They discovered a pocketknife concealed in a window frame. Apparently, Misenar intended to take his own life in the event he was convicted. Instead, the knife was taken away. He was sentenced to the State Penitentiary at Jackson the following day by the judge.

He was then brought through the town by the officers, amid streets filled with onlookers. He had to be assisted from one train to another, as his legs wobbled like a rag doll. He was described by the papers as "a most repulsive, dejected looking creature," when he departed Coldwater.

One year after being sent to the Michigan State Prison, he was transferred to the state insane asylum in Kalamazoo. Within a few years, however, he was again back in Jackson in prison serving his sentence of hard labor for life.

He was given a conditional pardon by Governor Chase Osborn in December 1911. In 1918, he was taken to court by his now ex-wife Daisy and required by the judge to pay alimony to her.

17

# THE DEADLY PORRIDGE OF MARY SANDERSON (1898)

*A very sensational case that reads like a dime novel story. If the charges against Mrs. Rudolphus Sanderson are proven true…she will be proven one of the coolest, most calculating and depraved woman criminals on record.*
—Battle Creek Moon, *October 10, 1898*

## RUDOLPHUS SANDERSON

Rudolphus Sanderson was born in the town of Milton, in Chittenden County, Vermont, in May 1818. His father was Levi Sanderson, a man of Irish descent. His mother was Sally Bean Sanderson, who was born in Nova Scotia and was of Scottish decent.

Rudolphus was brought up on his father's farm, attending the common school of Milton for his education. At age eighteen, he became a salesman in a mercantile store. A few years afterward, he bought his own store in Milton. He owned that business until he moved to Michigan in 1853.

During his time in Vermont, he served in the state legislature for two terms. In 1849, he married Ruth Adams, whose father was a lawyer and prominent citizen of Vermont. Together they would have two children, both of whom died at a young age. In later years, Rudolphus and Ruth adopted a young girl named Belle and raised her as their own.

When Rudolphus eventually moved to Michigan, he settled on a farm in Newton Township. Following his passion for serving the community, he was elected as Newton Township supervisor in 1861 and held that position for nine years.

In 1865, he was elected to the Michigan legislature, and in 1873 he was elected again. He later moved to Battle Creek and settled into a home at 98 East Main Street while managing the operations of his farm remotely. After this, he ran for and was elected to serve a term as an alderman of the First Ward in Battle Creek.

Rudolphus was a man who enjoyed being involved in shaping his community and considered public office to be an important public trust. For this reason, he became highly respected within the Battle Creek Community and around Calhoun County. He had

Mrs. Rudolphus Sanderson.

Mary Sanderson illustration, 1898. *From the Battle Creek Moon.*

also become a director of the City Bank. In the 1880 City Directory of Battle Creek, he was listed as a farmer and a capitalist.

Ruth Sanderson, his wife, passed away in 1896 at the age of sixty-nine. A short while after this, Belle, his adopted daughter, passed away in 1897 following an illness at the age of thirty-one. Rudolphus was seventy-nine years old and alone for the first time in his life. He was also a wealthy man, with property in Battle Creek, along with the farm he still owned in Newton Township.

# MARY BUTTERFIELD

Mary Butterfield grew up in Baraboo, Sauk County, Wisconsin, and was the third-eldest daughter of Harry Butterfield, a retired farmer who had been one of the early pioneers of the county. Mary was described as a blonde-haired young lady of medium build who developed a reputation as a flirt in her teens.

Rudolphus Sanderson, circa 1850. *Historical Society of Battle Creek.*

In 1893, at twenty-one years old, she became engaged to a prominent businessman in Sauk County. That year, Chicago was hosting the World's Columbian Exposition, known as the World's Fair. Together with other young people from the area, she and her fiancé visited the Windy City.

While there, she flirted with some of the other young Chicago men she encountered with her friends, going off with one of the new boys she met. When the excursion was over, her fiancé returned to Baraboo alone. Mary, however, remained in Chicago several weeks, staying with her new interest. When she finally returned to Wisconsin, her engagement was broken off. She worked as an assistant to a tailor for a few years and then moved to Battle Creek, Michigan, to seek training to become a nurse.

In 1897, Mary Butterfield, twenty-six years old, was working as an in-home nurse for an older woman on Rittenhouse Avenue. She told acquaintants she was in love with a young doctor who had just gotten out of school in Marquette and supposedly became engaged.

However, he had no money—nor did she, since she came from a large family of eight children in Wisconsin. Thus it would be a long time before they could be married, as neither had the means.

One day, she became acquainted with a neighbor woman next door to the client she was working for as a nurse. Through the neighbor, she heard of the death of Rudolphus Sanderson's adopted daughter, Belle. It was later believed by many that she conceived of an idea to resolve her financial problems when she heard of Mr. Sanderson losing his only remaining heir.

She asked the neighbor to write a letter of condolence to Mr. Sanderson on her behalf. The neighbor agreed, but when her husband came home and she told him of the request, he forbade her to do so, stating it was improper.

Whether this neighbor or another wrote the letter for Mary is not entirely known. Such a letter was eventually written to Rudolphus Sanderson. It was through this letter that she finally met him, with a formal introduction.

During this time, Nellie Wheeler, the niece of Mr. Sanderson, was keeping house for him. Her father was Onyx Adams, the brother of the former Ruth Adams, Rudolphus's deceased wife. She observed Mary Butterfield making calls at the home to see Mr. Sanderson, and she informed her father of what was going on. Onyx, together with his brother Jasper, concerned about Rudolph, intervened and succeeded for a time in breaking up Mary Butterfield's visits to Mr. Sanderson's home.

However, at a later time when Nellie was unable to work because she was sick, Mary Butterfield took advantage of her absence and resumed her visits to Mr. Sanderson.

Shortly after this, Mary attended Farrand Training School for nurses in Detroit, perhaps having gotten some money from her new friendship with Rudolphus. While at the nursing school, she corresponded with him to the result that he visited her in Detroit.

While there, together they crossed the border to Canada in Windsor. On July 6, 1898, they were married. Rudolphus was eighty years old, and his new wife Mary was twenty-seven.

# NEWLYWEDS

The newlywed couple returned to Battle Creek the next day and began boarding together in the Sanderson home. Rudolphus's two brothers in Chicago and the Adams family were shocked—not only at the unannounced and unexpected marriage but also of the marked age difference between the two. Concerns abounded that Mary was a swindler.

The remains of that summer and into early autumn, the couple lived together in their home on East Main Street. On Saturday evening, September 3, Rudolphus began feeling ill. He was found unconscious on the floor. Mrs. Sanderson called her hired girl for help but did not notify any of the neighbors. Together, the women carried Mr. Sanderson to his bed. When Mary tumbled her elderly husband over on the bed, she exclaimed, "Lay there now, will you."

And he did lay there. The neighbors reported being awakened to Rudolphus's piteous calls for "Mary, Mary…" echoing in the hours after sunset throughout the night. After a time, they saw lights moving around in the house and saw the silhouette of Mary come downstairs, where she had left him in one of the rooms all alone. No physician was called until eleven o'clock the next morning, when they sent for Dr. Jervis Wattles, who was called out of a church service.

Jasper Adams, hearing the news of Rudolphus's illness, came to see him on Sunday and remained by his side until he passed away in the early hours of Tuesday, September 6.

On the morning that Rudolphus passed away, Jasper Adams sent word to Fred A. Allwardt, the cashier at the City Bank, of which Mr. Sanderson had been the director. He asked Allwardt to take charge of Sanderson's papers, which he consented to do, provided Mrs. Sanderson agreed. When Mary came into the room, the matter was suggested to her, and she consented. Mary produced a key to Mr. Sanderson's locked private secretary and took out all of the papers within, handing them over to Mr. Allwardt, who deposited them at the bank.

The only Will and Testament found within the documents was dated in 1882. This willed $2,000 to his stepdaughter, Belle, when she would become an adult, and $3,000 at his death. All the property would go to his first wife, Ruth Sanderson. The witnesses to this will in writing were Mr. Allwardt and another man, R. Kingman, who was deceased. As both Ruth Sanderson and Belle Sanderson were dead, in the state of Michigan at the time, the property would then go to the natural heirs. According to this description in the law, the only legal remaining heir was Mary.

The mystery that lingered in everyone's mind who knew Rudolphus was, why he as a banker did not make a second will. He had been known to be a shrewd and careful businessman. He would not have failed to make a second will knowing that the heirs in the original one were no longer living.

A lot of speculation abounded about the existence of a second will and Mary having destroyed it. The old will left the property in better shape for her to receive everything, as she was ultimately his only heir. If a second will was written, could it have left less money for her? She did have the key to his private papers and probably knew the contents.

# A WITNESS COMES FORWARD

Rudolphus was buried at Oak Hill Cemetery within a few days of his passing, as was customary during that time. Mary, the Adamses and friends from the community attended.

It was right after the funeral service that a Scottish woman who had worked for the Sandersons as a domestic servant, Marie Robertson, approached Ela Adams, the wife of Jasper Adams. She claimed that she had witnessed Mary Sanderson put ground glass in Rudolphus's porridge and that she had been administering this to him for two weeks prior to his death.

The news of this shocking story soon spread, and Sheriff William Stone was notified of Marie Robertson's statements. He summoned Marie to his office, where she recounted what she had witnessed. The sheriff then received permission from the township supervisor to disinter the remains of Mr. Sanderson.

The following day, without notifying Mary Sanderson, the sheriff, in the company of the undertaker and two deputies, went to Oak Hill Cemetery and disinterred the body. The remains were placed in a wagon and taken to the hearse barn at the undertaker's office.

When they arrived there, a jury was sworn in by the sheriff to witness the proceedings. In front of the jury and Justice Harry Lewis, the casket was opened and the remains placed on a stretcher. A doctor was present and removed the stomach and intestines, placing them in a clean jar, which was then sealed with wax.

# ARRESTED

The jar was escorted by the deputies to Ann Arbor, where it was tested in a laboratory at the University of Michigan. The test came back as positive for traces of ground glass within the stomach and intestines. Rumors began to circulate within the community that Mary Sanderson was going to be arrested.

When rumors had reached her of a pending arrest, Mary employed an attorney named Nathan Briggs. However, after a week, she verbally informed him that she did not desire his services. She discovered he had been a friend of her late husband. Briggs sent her word that he desired her to put her request for termination of services in writing, and she refused. She told him that she "was not going to give him a sample of her handwriting" to be used against her. She then hired another attorney, William Crosby, to represent her.

Mary Sanderson wanted cashier Allwardt from the City Bank to be appointed administrator of her husband's estate, but he refused to assume the responsibility. She then demanded the copy of his will be released to her.

He refused to let her have it, instead forwarding it to the probate judge for safekeeping. The probate judge then appointed Charles Thomas, another local attorney, to be the administrator of the estate.

During this time, Mary's father, Harry Butterfield, arrived in town and chastised cashier Allwardt when he refused to release the will to Mary. Tensions between Mary Sanderson's family and the Adamses, the relatives of Rudolphus's first wife, Ruth, were just beginning.

Onyx Adams had a note stating he had loaned Mr. Sanderson $1,300, and this document had mysteriously disappeared and was not found among the papers given to Allwardt.

Fearing arrest, Mary became desperate for money. She sold her interest in the entire Sanderson estate to a man named Gavin Ritchie for $6,000, who paid her $100 down as a deposit. He immediately took possession of her house on East Main Street.

She then left the city for a few days. When she returned on Friday, she had found two other brothers, Edward and George Stringham, who would give her the $6,000 cash. They then approached Ritchie with $500 to relinquish his claim to the estate, which he did. A week later, Jasper Adams purchased the claims from the Stringham brothers.

The Saturday following her husband's death, Mary Sanderson was arrested and charged with murder. The funeral, disinterment, investigation and her legal challenges had all happened in the same week leading up to her being taken into custody.

# The Trial

The trial of Mary Sanderson began on October 24, continuing through December 23. The presiding judge, Justice Henry Lewis, became ill in the middle of the proceedings, which delayed the trial for several weeks.

Outwardly, the case against Mary Sanderson appeared quite damning. However, the core of the prosecuting attorney's case included the evidence of the glass found by the lab in Ann Arbor and the testimony of Marie Robertson. Both were circumstantial.

When Marie testified at trail, she stated that she had worked for Mr. Sanderson for over a year. She claimed that about three weeks prior to the death of Mr. Sanderson, she had been working in the kitchen and taken ill. Mrs. Sanderson had offered to help prepare Mr. Sanderson's meals, allowing her to rest on a chair in the kitchen while she prepared his porridge.

She testified that she witnessed Mrs. Sanderson take a glass tray down into the basement and heard glass breaking. She then looked down the stairs into the basement, and saw her grinding the glass in a coffee mill. Later, she saw her return with fragments of a white powder on a soup plate and then mix it into the porridge.

She claimed that she had witnessed Mrs. Sanderson mix this into the porridge of Mr. Sanderson for two weeks, never telling anyone for fear they would not believe her. Marie maintained at trial that if she as a domestic servant had told anyone, Mrs. Sanderson would simply deny it and she would be fired.

William Crosby, Mary Sanderson's defense attorney, cross-examined Marie while she was on the stand. He challenged her on how she knew it was glass that Mrs. Sanderson had brought up from the basement and not something else. Marie stood by her claims, but Crosby challenged her every utterance.

Additionally, Crosby made a point to challenge her on why she did not tell. Marie maintained it was the reasons she stated, that no one would believe her. There is some truth to this claim. During the Victorian era, domestic servants were often considered a lower class of society. If one told stories of their employers, they were not likely to find work again if they were released from employment. Speaking out, even if observing criminal conduct, had potential long-term consequences.

Crosby was able to make it appear to the jury, however, that Marie was perhaps exaggerating or not being entirely truthful. Following his cross-examination of Marie, he presented to the court that the entire case was founded on money. He claimed that the desire for money from the Adams family in the estate of Mr. Sanderson was what drove the proceedings. He implied that when Onyx and Jasper Adams had heard Marie Robertson's story, they used their influence to manipulate the sheriff's office. He claimed that it was the Adams family behind the charges; they wanted Mary Sanderson committed to life in prison so that they could claim the estate.

Crosby then presented testimony from people who had overheard Onyx and Jasper discussing money and the estate.

The prosecuting attorney then put Marie Robertson back on the stand and continued to question her.

Before he could get very far, Crosby entered a motion to have that stage of the proceeding dismissed based on three reasons, stating that the first was because the prosecution had not allowed examination of all of the witnesses, specifically Robertson, before the trial. Robertson was initially detained as a suspect in the crime, and this fact had been withheld from the defense. And finally, the presiding justice, Judge Lewis, had issued the order for disinterment, been present at the disinterment of the body of Mr. Sanderson and witnessed the autopsy. Therefore, he could not preside over the case and was now a material witness.

The prosecuting attorney objected to the motion, declaring it was entirely without foundation. Justice Lewis ruled then that the trial would continue, overruling Mr. Crosby's motion. The gravity of these claims, despite being overruled, would weigh on the minds of the jury.

Marie Robertson was again put on the stand by the prosecution. When it came time again for Crosby to re-question her, he again pressed on why she did not tell neighbors. Marie again maintained she did, at the funeral, but Crosby challenged her over and over on why she had not done so before.

He also questioned Marie on her knowledge of powders and hair products, trying to shed doubt on her ability to ascertain the difference between common flour, hair products and ground glass. He also ruthlessly asked her if she had ever told anyone that Mr. Sanderson deserved what he got because he was a fool for marrying Mary. This Marie emphatically denied.

Following this exchange, a lively debate between the prosecuting attorney and the defense attorney followed, during which the prosecution demanded that the defense ease his continual frivolous line of questioning of the witness.

## THE VERDICT

This battle between the attorneys continued into late December. In the closing arguments, the prosecuting attorney stated to the jury: "If Marie Robertson told the truth, then the respondent is guilty, and she had no motive for telling a lie. She was compelled to come here and testify, and had done so against her own interests. Her testimony was corroborated by reliable witnesses."

Defense attorney Crosby followed with his address to the jury by painting Marie Robertson in anything but a favorable light. In essence, the trial came down to material evidence of ground glass found in the victim and the testimony of Marie Robertson.

The prosecution and defense finally rested on December 23. The jury went into deliberation at eight o'clock in the evening. At one minute past midnight, four hours later, they rapped on the jury door, and the foreman announced that a verdict had been reached. Mary Sanderson gazed at the twelve men intently with a forlorn look on her face as the usual questions to the foreman were asked by the presiding judge. Then the foreman announced the verdict of "not guilty."

Acquitted, Mary Sanderson was released. The newspapers reported that the large audience present applauded vigorously. She fell into her father's arms, weeping, and then stepped up to the jury, shaking each one of their hands, thanking them.

## Questions Unanswered

The trial of Mary Sanderson and its outcome are perplexing. Did this verdict come down to simply there not being any more evidence of Mary Sanderson committing the crime? Or was it a societal flaw of the Victorian era in which domestic servants were not regarded as credible witnesses because they were considered a lower, uneducated class? In contrast to this consideration was the fact that Mary Sanderson had only recently been Mary Butterfield, who was essentially in the same class as Marie Robertson.

It is possible the decision to exonerate Mary Sanderson from wrongdoing simply came down to having William Crosby as her attorney. He certainly was able to convince the jury, and get them to look past the fact that ground glass was indeed found in Rudolphus Sanderson's stomach and intestines. Someone had caused him to ingest this, as the man never prepared his own food.

The press aggressively researched Mary Sanderson's backstory. They interviewed friends and family in Wisconsin and also the people who knew her from her brief stay at the nursing school in Detroit, as well as members of the local community. Mary Sanderson did indeed have a track record of manipulating men. She had also been seen to flirt with the deputies and the sheriff while in custody and was always making flattering comments about them when given access to the press.

Mary had married a man almost three times her age, and he died, leaving a large estate, less than six months after they were married. It is not surprising that neighbors and family were suspicious. His brothers Lucius Sanderson, an attorney from Chicago, and Charles Sanderson of Milwaukee, however, believed she was innocent.

If it were not Mary Sanderson who killed her husband, who did? Marie Robertson had nothing to gain from killing him; she was not included in any will. How else did ground glass find its way into the porridge of Rudolphus Sanderson? All indications pointed to Mary; however, one can also see the jury's perspective on the point of reasonable doubt.

Another thought to consider is that the jury, after two months of trial, with a long delay because of the illness of Justice Lewis in the middle of it, was released into deliberation the day before Christmas Eve. Was this a factor?

Mary appeared to benefit the most from her husband's death. When examining the existing will, she was set to inherit an estate estimated to be worth $25,000 at the time, mostly in property. Some other estimates claimed the estate may have been as high as $100,000. However, there was a problem. She had already sold her rights to the property to pay for her legal defense.

## Lawsuits

In June 1899, Mary Sanderson filed suit against Gavin Ritchie, Edward and George Stringham, Jasper and his wife, Ela Adams, and also Lucius Sanderson, one of the surviving brothers of Rudolphus. All had filed claims on the estate, and Mary was fighting for her percentage.

Ritchie and the Stringham brothers had been the men she sold her interests to. Jasper and Ela were named in the suit, as she claimed they caused her first trial to be held in order to get her convicted and acquire the estate, which caused her to sell her interests at below their value to pay for a defense. Also, Jasper had since purchased half of the estate from the Stringham brothers. Lucius Sanderson from Chicago was included because he had stepped in and filed a claim on his brother's estate. Onyx Adams was not named in the suit, as he had passed away since the original trial.

Mary lost the case and was not rewarded any property. She then appealed it to the Michigan State Supreme Court. The conspiracy claim was dismissed by the court, but they did make only one change to the earlier ruling, which yielded a payment to Mary of one hundred dollars from the Stringham brothers, due to a mathematical error discovered.

# New Charges, New Trial

The county prosecutor was not done with his attempts to bring justice for Rudolphus Sanderson. In January 1899, Mary Sanderson was again brought up on charges regarding the death of her husband. She was confined to the jail in Marshall pending her trial. Having been acquitted of murder, this time she was charged with attempted murder.

Following a long continuance, the trial was eventually held in December 1899. All of the details of the previous trial were again brought up.

By this time, $8,000 in life insurance money had been discovered in Rudolphus's papers, and the insurance companies were withholding payment, pending the outcome of the trial. William Crosby represented Mary again, and this time he even put Judge Lewis from the original trial on the stand as a witness.

Marie Robertson was again brought up to testify and this time entered additional testimony alleging that Mary had slept with other men while Rudolphus was still alive, stating she was instructed not to talk about it.

In the end, this trial lasted about a month. Again, the jury was sent out for deliberation on December 23. Like before they came back with an acquittal on the grounds the prosecution had not convinced them beyond a reasonable doubt.

Rudolphus Sanderson plot marker. *Author's collection.*

# THE ESTATE

In April 1900, the estate of Rudolphus Sanderson was finally settled and determined by the probate court. Mary Sanderson was awarded half of the estate, and the rest was divided among Lucius Sanderson and several other nieces and nephews who had filed a claim. Mary, however, had already sold her rights to the property, which were now owned by Jasper Adams. She gained no property from the probate court decision.

In October 1901, now living in Grand Rapids, Mary Sanderson again filed a declaration in the courts alleging she was taken advantage of and the property was taken away from her at a time of distress. She was requesting the courts set aside the deeds and return them to her ownership, citing distress at the time of transfer, claiming she was incompetent to sign.

The case was finally heard in the courts in March 1902. Mary Sanderson lost again. She appealed the ruling to the Michigan Supreme Court in December 1902. The case was denied by the Michigan Supreme Court, which brought an end to the saga of Mary Sanderson's pursuit of her husband's property.

# BIBLIOGRAPHY

## Introduction

Anderson, Janna Quitney. *Imagining the Internet: Personalities, Predictions, Perspectives*. Lanham, MD: Rowman and Littlefield, 2005.

*Evening News* (Battle Creek, MI). January 1, 1916.

Farhud, Dariush D., and Mrjan Zarif Yeganeh. "A Brief History of Human Blood Groups." *Iranian Journal of Public Health* 42, no. 1 (2013): 1–6. National Institute of Health, January 1, 2013. https://www.ncbi.nlm.nih.gov/pmc/articles/PMC3595629/.

Historical Association U.K. "Victorian Britain: A Brief History." https://www.history.org.uk.

Lawyers.com. "Hearsay, a Brief History." *Lawyer Blogs*, April 18, 2015. https://blogs.lawyers.com.

Morton, Alison. "The Female Crime: Gender, Class and Female Criminality in Victorian Representations of Poisoning." *Midlands Historical Review* 5 (2021). http://www.midlandshistoricalreview.com.

National Forensic Science Technology Center. "Simplified Guide to Crime Scene Photography." June 27, 2012. https://www.forensicsciencesimplified.org/photo/Photography.pdf.

O'Brien, James. *The Scientific Sherlock Holmes: Cracking the Case with Science and Forensics*. New York: Oxford University Press, 2013.

*Right on Track: A History of the Railroads in Eaton County, Michigan*. Eaton County Historical Commission, 2019.

Swisher, Clarice. *Victorian England: Turning Points in World History*. New York: Greenhaven, 2000.

# Note

For a complete bibliography on chapters 1–17, visit michaeldelaware.com.

# INDEX

# W

# Y

# Z

# ABOUT THE AUTHOR

Michael Delaware is an Arizona native who left home at age eighteen. He lived fifteen years in Georgia, where he worked as a craftsman, artist, salesperson, manager and owner of a stained and decorative glass door and window business. He moved to Ann Arbor, Michigan, in 1999 and later to Battle Creek from 2001 to the present.

Raised by a father who was not only a hardworking restaurant systems installer but also a storyteller and a mother who was an avid reader and a librarian, he has long valued the importance of learning about the past and telling a good story. Throughout the many places he has lived, he has been fascinated with reading and learning about local history.

In 2010, he started a YouTube channel but did not align his passion for history and video production until 2020, when he began producing local videos on the past. In 2022, he launched his podcast *Tales of Southwest Michigan's Past*. He is passionate about researching forgotten stories from the Victorian era and is known for his video programs on local cemetery, landmark and biographical history.

He has also been involved with community improvement projects, including serving on the committee that built the Home Run Dog Park in 2019 in Battle Creek, and served as a design consultant on the construction of the Springfield Dog Park, which opened in 2022 in Springfield, Michigan.

In January 2022, he joined the board of the Battle Creek Regional History Museum and volunteers his time serving as the marketing director and promoting events, fundraising and writing programs for the organization.

He also lectures on local historical topics and enjoys promoting regional museums, history authors and organizations on his podcast and YouTube channel to encourage others to learn about and take interest in preserving local and regional history.

*Visit us at*
www.historypress.com
·········································································